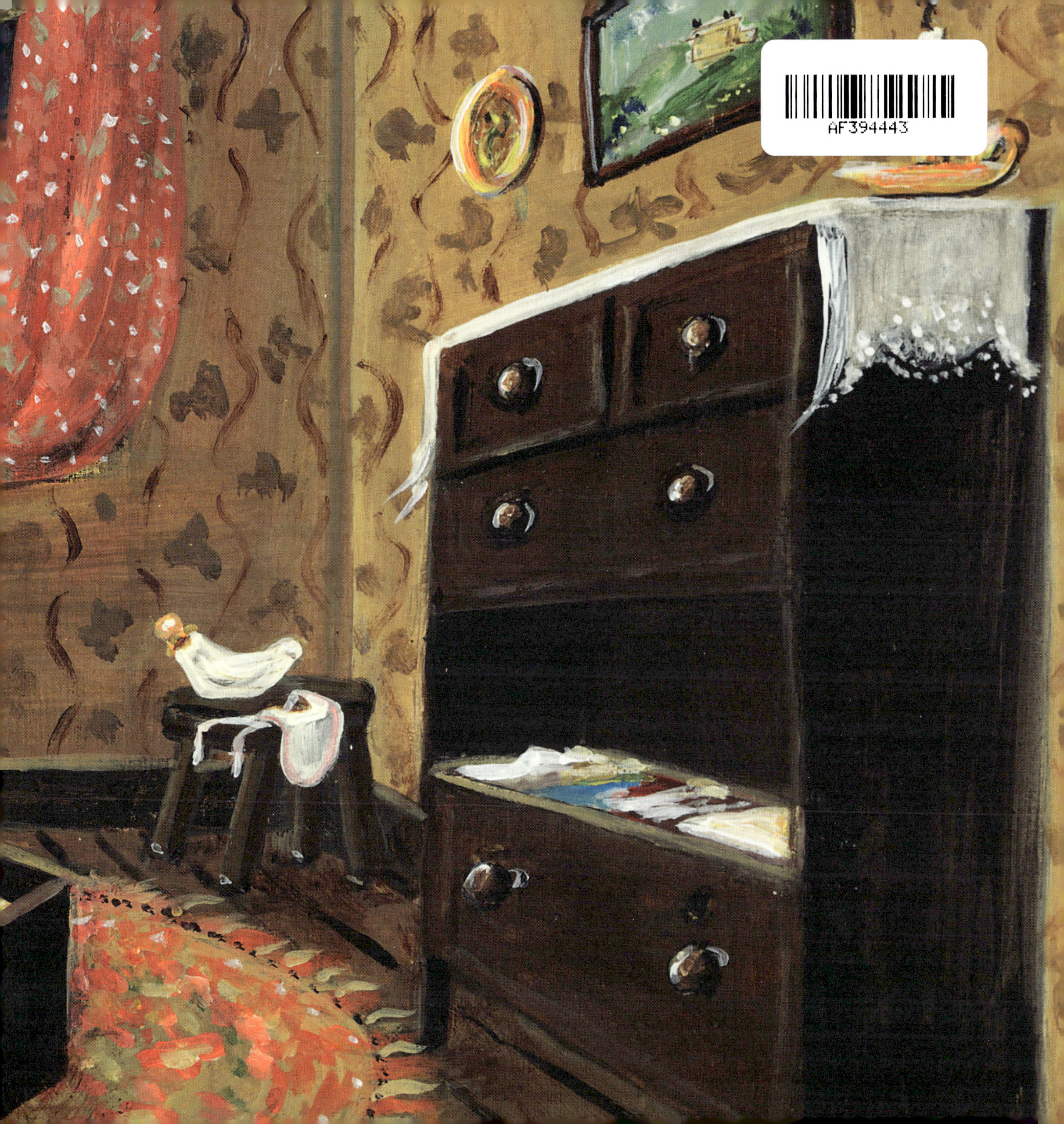
AF394443

EARTH MEADOW

Earth Meadow: Paintings by Eironwy Llewellyn
Published in Great Britain in 2023 by Bird Eye Books,
an imprint of Graffeg Limited.

Text and photographs by Eironwy and Sara Llewellyn
copyright © 2023. Designed and produced by Graffeg
Limited copyright © 2023.

Graffeg Limited, 24 Stradey Park Business Centre,
Mwrwg Road, Llangennech, Llanelli, Carmarthenshire,
SA14 8YP, Wales, UK. www.graffeg.com.

Sara Llewellyn is hereby identified as the author
of this work in accordance with section 77
of the Copyright, Designs and Patents Act 1988.

A CIP Catalogue record for this book is available
from the British Library.

The publisher gratefully acknowledges the financial
support of this book by the Books Council of Wales.
www.gwales.com.

ISBN 9781802584455

Printed in China TT15122022

1 2 3 4 5 6 7 8 9

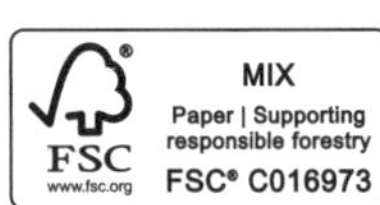

More about Earth Meadow online

High-quality prints of the paintings
from EarthMeadowPrints.Etsy.com

EARTH MEADOW

Paintings by Eironwy Llewellyn

Sara Llewellyn

BIRD EYE BOOKS

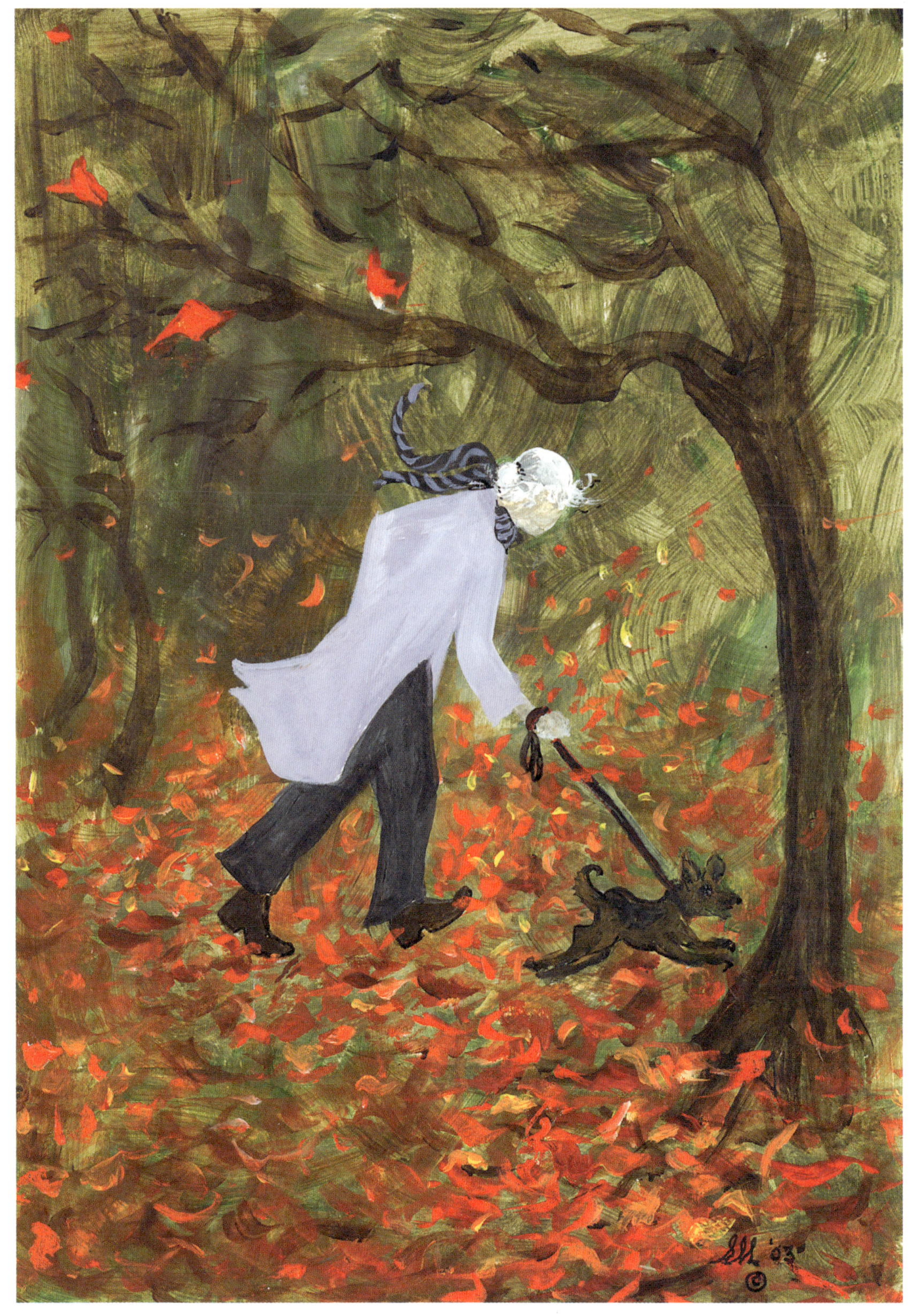

CONTENTS

Left: Self-portrait sketch, 2003.

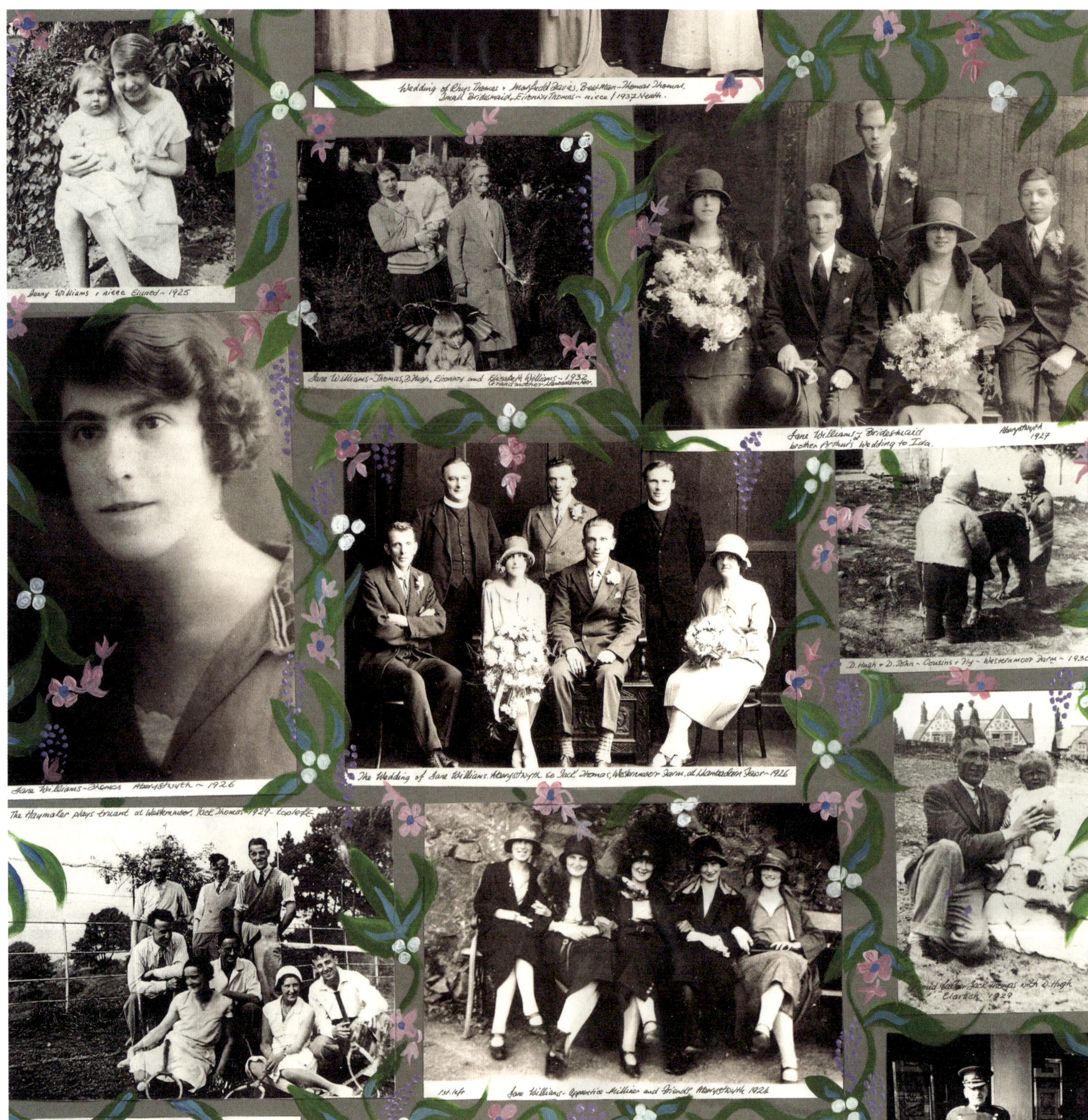

Jenny Williams + niece Eluned ~ 1925

Wedding of Rhys Thomas + Maxfield Davis, Best Man~Thomas Thomas, Small Bridesmaid, Eleanor Thomas~ niece / 1937. Neath.

Jane Williams~Thomas, D.Hugh, Eleanor and Elizabeth Williams ~ 1932. Grandmother Llanwddau Fawr.

Jane Williams 3 Bridesmaid / brother Arthur's Wedding to Ida. Aberystwyth 1927

Jane Williams~Thomas Aberystwyth ~ 1926

The Wedding of Jane Williams. Aberystwyth to Jack Thomas, Westernmoor Farm. at Llanbadarn Fawr ~ 1926

D.Hugh + D.John ~ Cousins + Fly ~ Westernmoor Farm ~ 1930

Proud Father Jack Thomas with D.Hugh Clarach 1929

The Haymaker plays truant at Westernmoor, Jack Thomas 1929~ top left.

1st. left — Jane Williams- Apprentice Milliner and Friends, Aberystwyth 1924

INTRODUCTION

It's an odd thing, discovering the first fourteen years of your mother's life in full colour and with so much written detail when she's not there anymore! So began my own Herculean task: to curate, collate, capture, compile and edit the prolific, bursting-at-the-seams work of Eironwy.

Painted retrospectively from memory whilst in her seventies, this collection presents a pictorial diary of a forgotten time from 1930-1944 of a Welsh childhood lived on the farm and by the sea.

I can sense in them her intense relief at dropping the pretence of her adult life – trying to be a good middle-class wife, mother, teacher, friend, enduring the boredom of conformity, the suffocation of her wild, free spirit.

A trained, highly skilled sculptor, here she was coming to the last stages of her life and giving two of her worn-out fingers, in all their workish glory, to the 'establishment' and deliberately painting in a contrived naïve style. Her dazzling chosen colour palettes and pelted brushstrokes are grounded in emphatic emotion pouring out of her very being – who she really was, at last revealed!

Producing this book has been heady stuff for me, the messenger of that surprising Welsh Mam of mine. The title, *Earth Meadow*, is my choice, an instinctive one for something simple on the surface but complex and layered, joyous and sometimes quite dark. The paintings and their accompanying stories have already resonated with thousands of individuals around the world, from different generations and all walks of life. Through *Earth Meadow*, I hope they will reach and be enjoyed by many more.

Sara Llewellyn

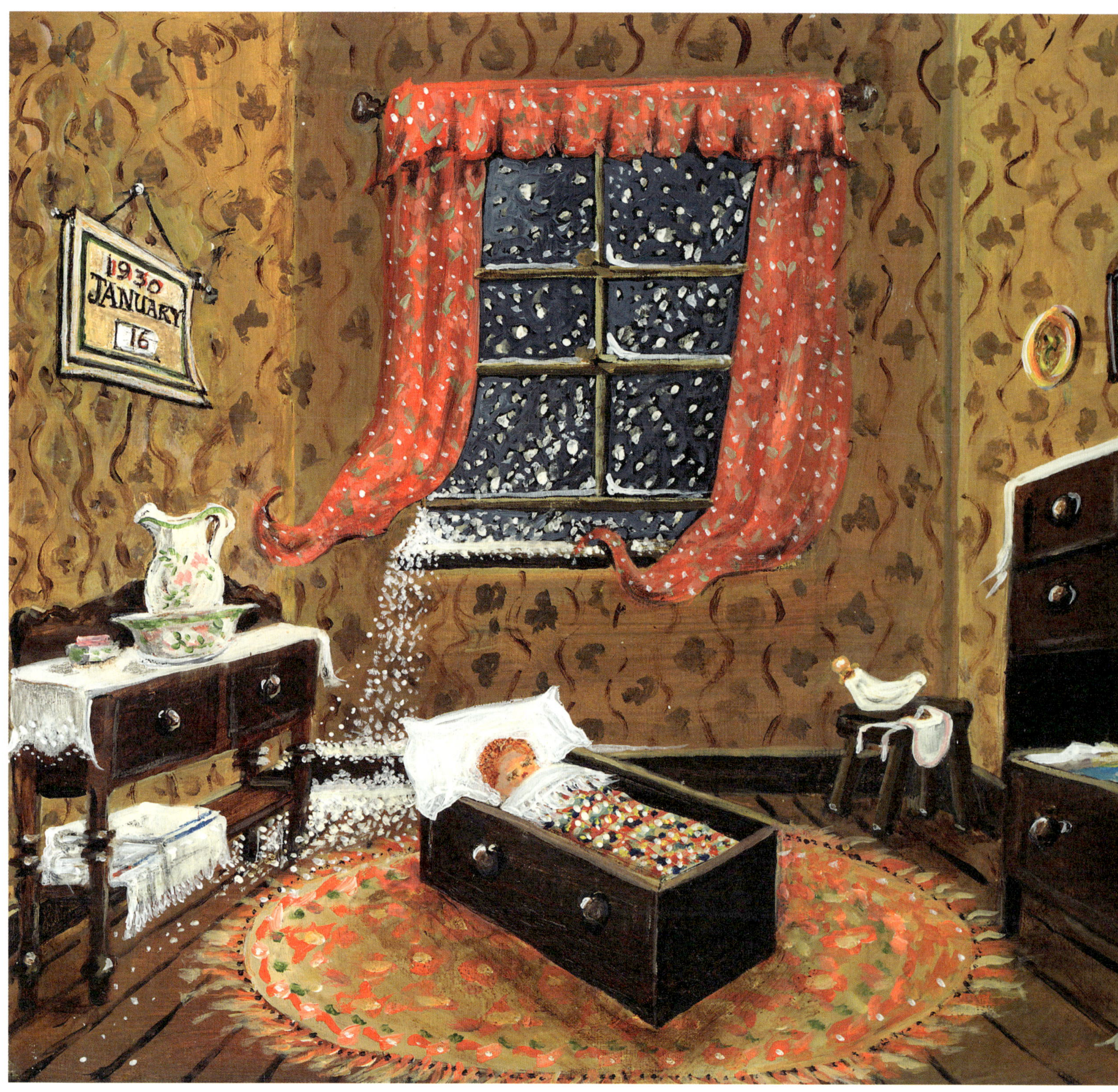
1930
JANUARY
16

BIRTHDAY

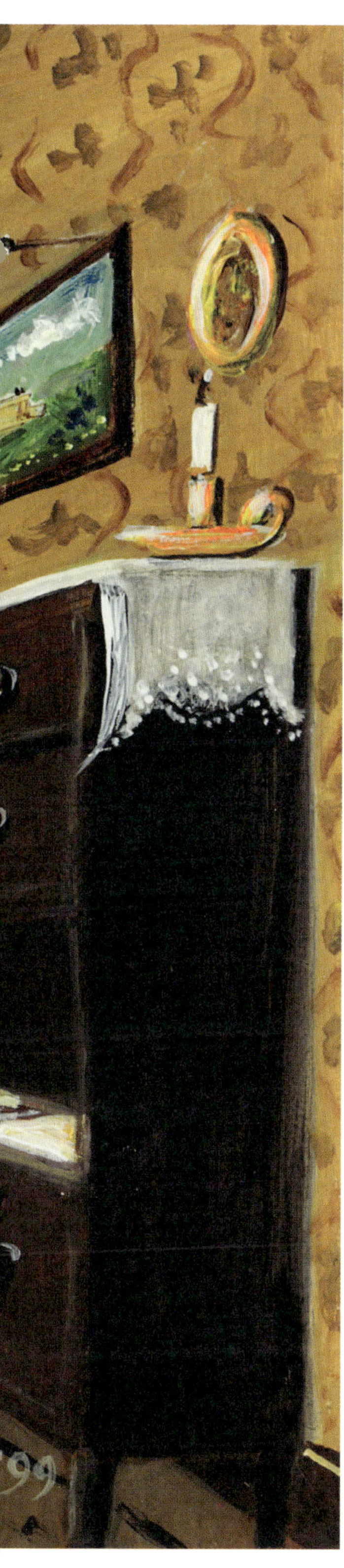

So here I am, a newborn baby asleep in a drawer borrowed from a chest of drawers, a makeshift cot. It is January and snowing. The house I am in belongs to a stranger – I have had to be farmed out to a woman nearby who has a baby of her own because my mother had a difficult delivery and was rushed to hospital from the house in which I was actually born, my maternal grandmother's, Mamam. That house is a tiny terraced house in a village near the wild coast.

My mother had travelled a hundred miles from her in-law's farm in order to have her baby in the only place a woman gets tender loving care, and that is in her own mother's home. On this occasion there was illness in the tiny house: Papa was being nursed in a bed which had been brought down to the front parlour, he having double pneumonia, while Mamam was blind with cataracts.

My merry spinster aunt also lived there and could not nurse a newborn baby as well. Hence the makeshift cot, the drawer, the glass feeding bottle with rubber teat and the absence of immediate doting family.

We all survived this crisis, apart from my mother rejecting me at birth, so goes the story, because I was born with carrot-red hair. The offending colour eventually fell out, my father's blond genes asserted themselves and my mother's maternal instincts were revived.

FILING HER NAILS

This is a scene in one of the downstairs rooms in Mamam and Papa's house by the coast. There's a nice brightly burning fire in the black-leaded grate with brass fender. In the scene is a table and chairs, and sitting on them is my dear Papa and a neighbour we called Aunty. I'm standing between Papa's knees and he's filing my fingernails with the sandpapered side of a matchbox – England's Glory, I think, or Swan Vestas.

He was gentle as a butterfly with my nails, so careful and wanting his grandchild's nails to be beautifully manicured, such a loving act to have done for me.
He checked us over, cousins all – and there were many – whenever we visited.

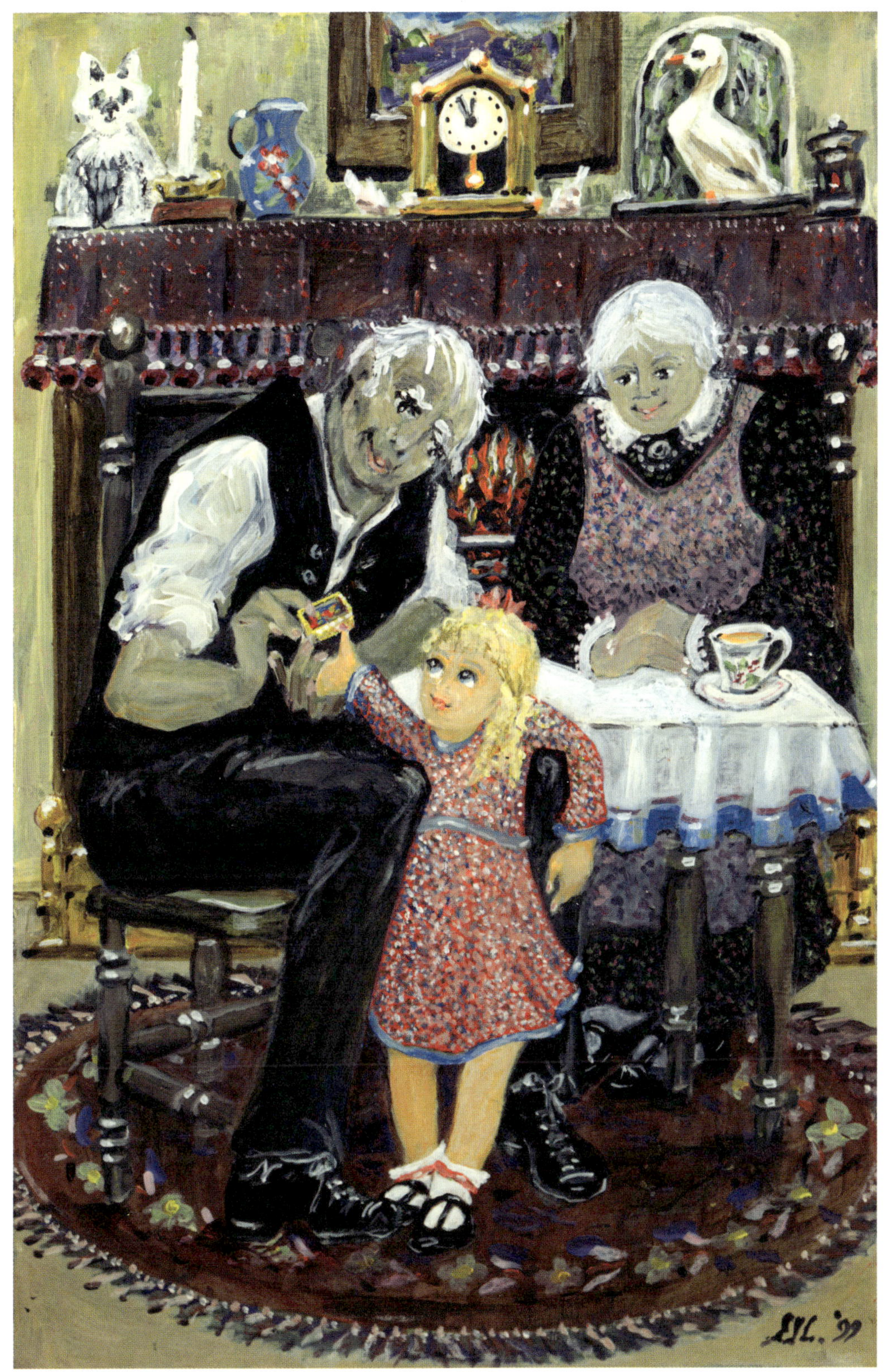

MILK DELIVERY

Soft voices wake me, speaking in Welsh, and I am leaning out of the window of the same terraced house, gazing down at the scene outside. It is early morning on a summer's day, the scent of sea air mingling with that of heavily green trees and tiny wildflowers growing in crevices everywhere. The slow drag of a fat little carthorse's hooves announces the arrival of Mr Jenkins the Milk, or it may have been Mr Jones the Milk. My merry spinster aunt is ordering extra, 'We've got our visitors here, Mr Jenkins!' She holds out two big china jugs for him to ladle warm, frothy milk into from churns high up on the cart. The milk is warm because it has not long left the body heat of Mr Jenkins' cows on his nearby farm. The cream has not settled yet, but when it does... '*Diolch yn fawr*, Mr Jenkins, *bore da*.' All speech was in Welsh, of course, the lovely fulsome northern Welsh which my father used to tease my mother about due to its broad vowels. She in turn would scoff back at his 'southy' accent. I grew up in a totally Welsh-speaking environment, on both sides of the family, so that when I started school I was sent back home for a term to be taught English. Thus, I learnt English via the newspaper cartoon Rupert Bear. My mother used to spread it out on the floor, and I would slowly begin to read and speak English. I loved the adventures of Rupert and his friends.

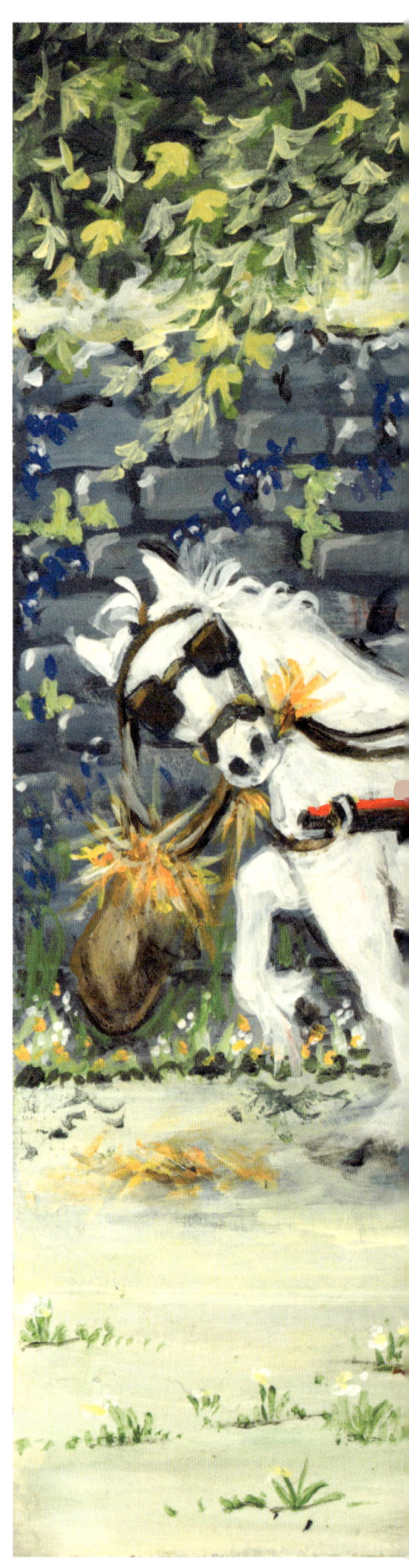

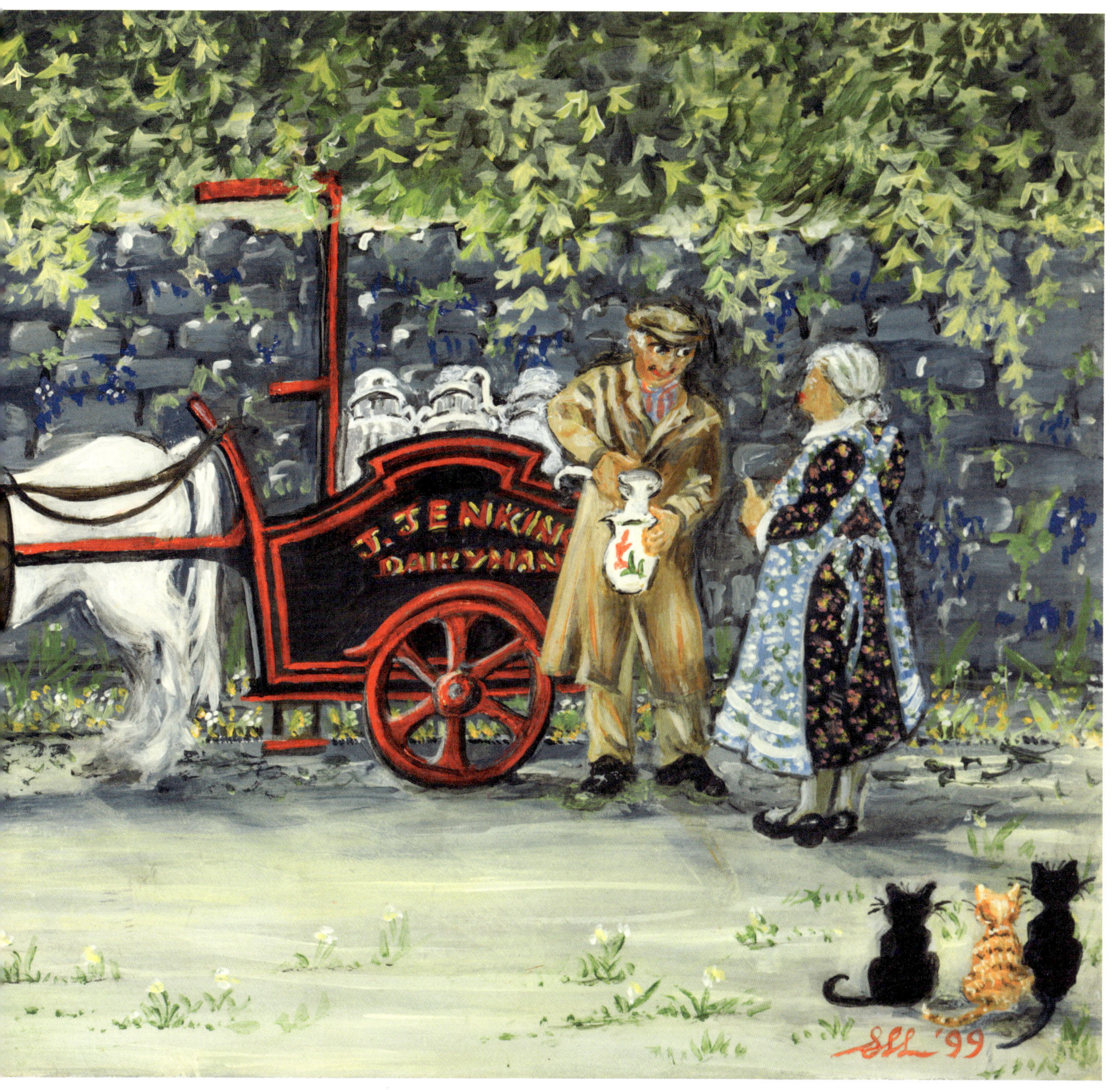

J. JENKINS
DAIRYMAN

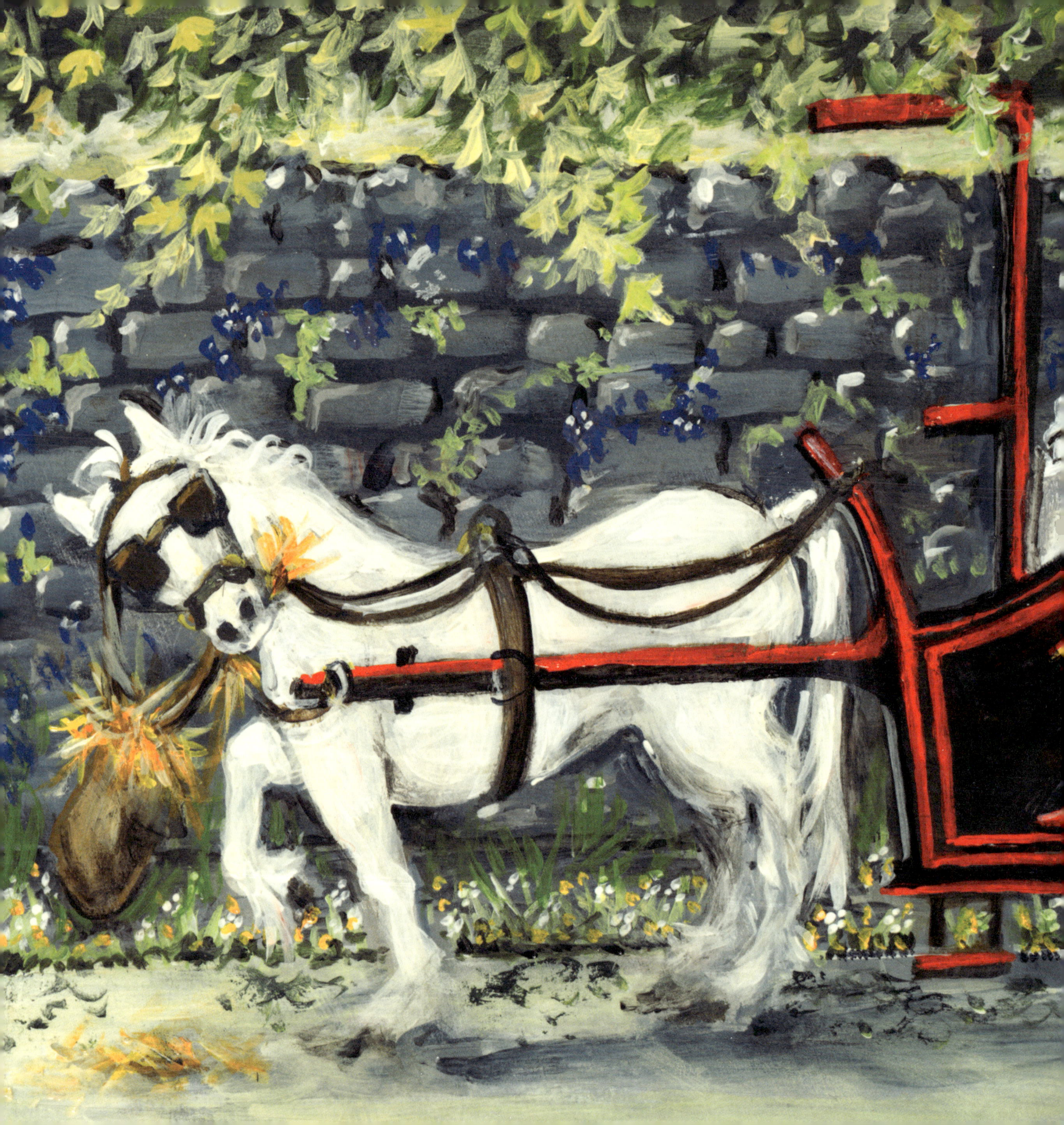

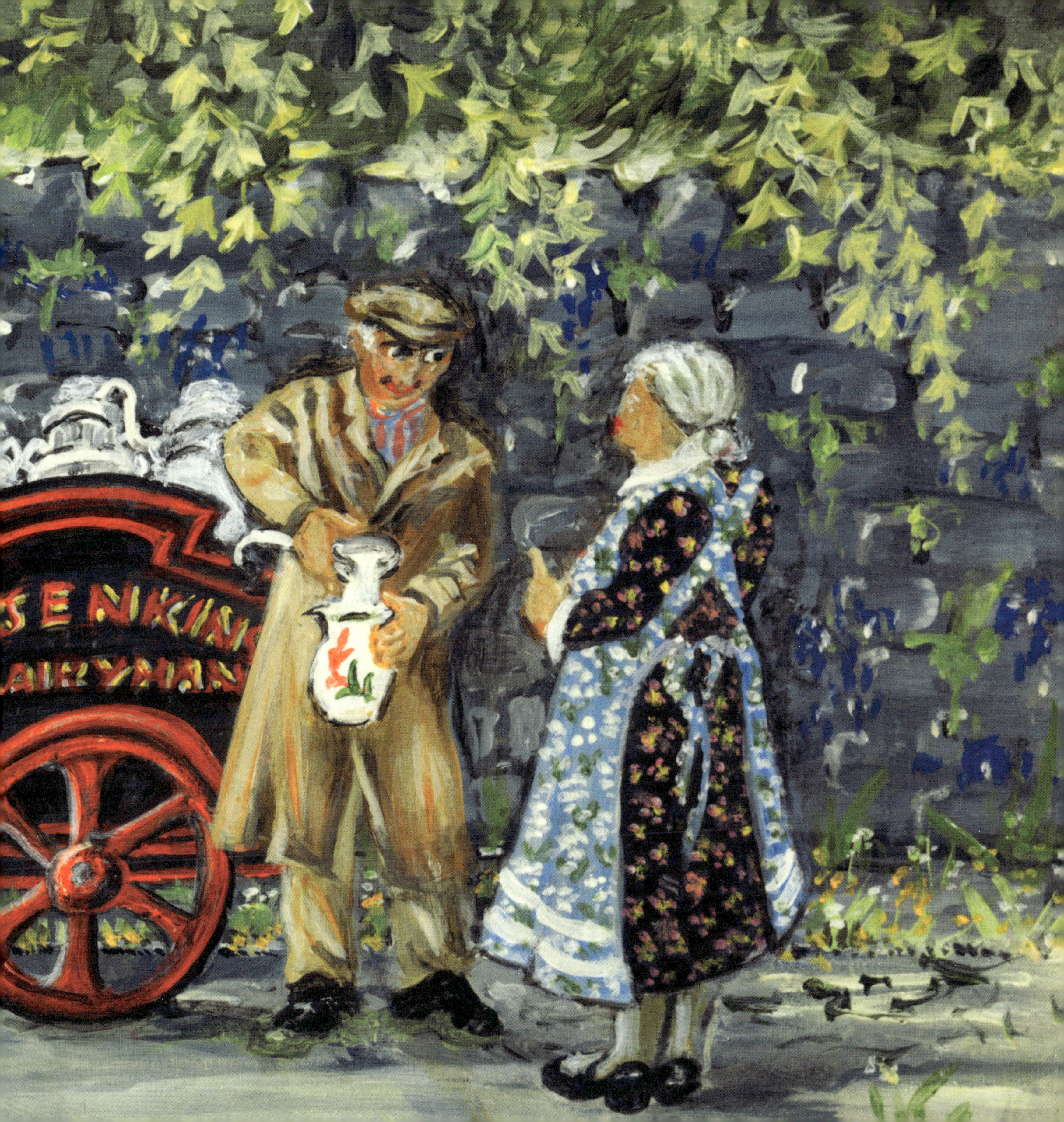

JENKINS
DAIRYMAN

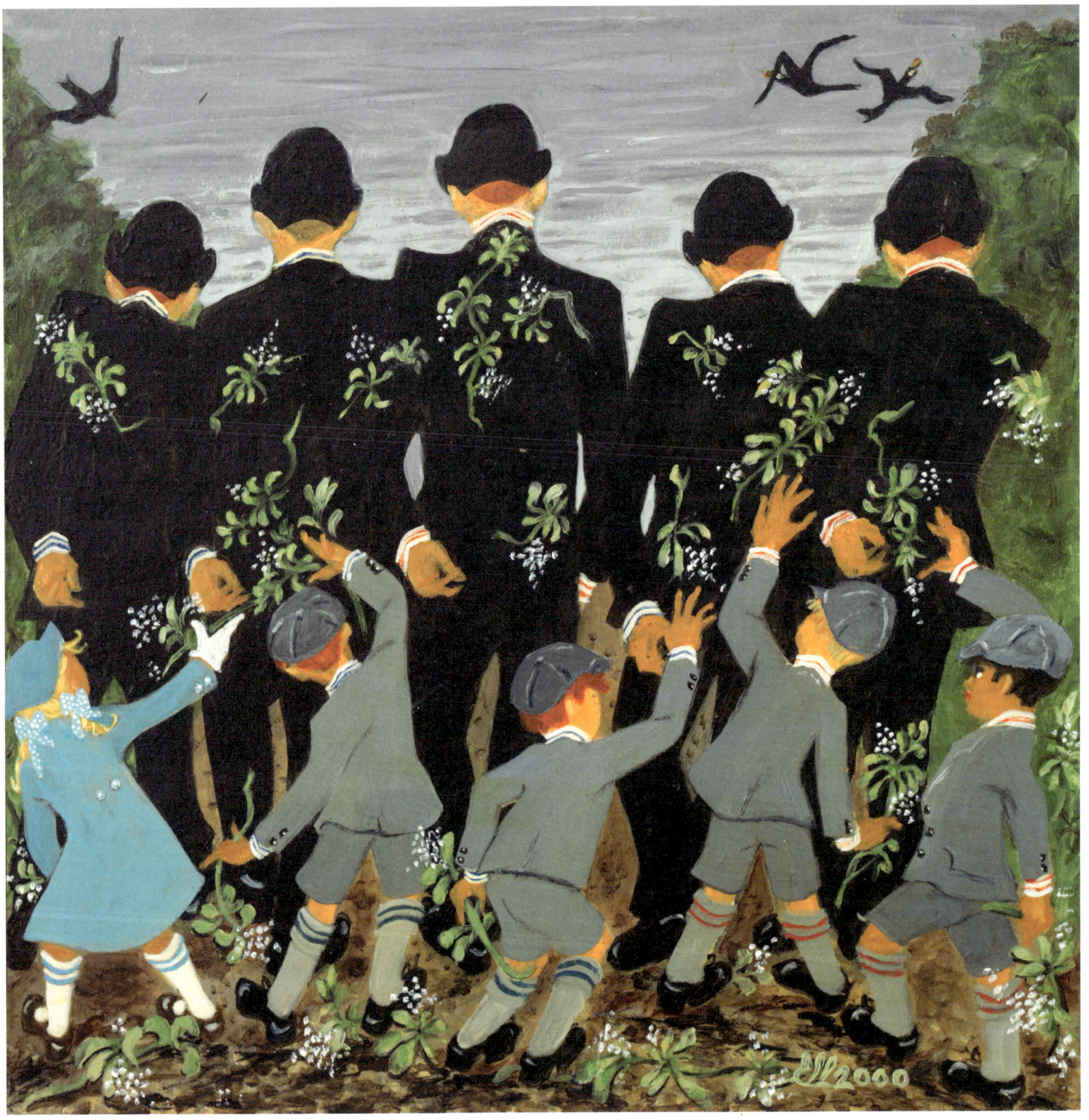

WALKING TO CHAPEL

This shows a family group walking along a lane which led from Mamgu's farm through the countryside to a small chapel. It is Sunday. I only went there a few times, but the uncles were regulars, dressed in their black serge Sunday suits, black bowler hats, clean, clean shirts and highly polished black boots. We, the gaggle of small cousins, five of us, would trail along behind in our very best clothes too, trying to be on our best behaviour – a short-lived possibility due to one particularly mischievous member – it was wiser to give in than to argue 'fair play' or common sense. Thus, in this scene the children have plucked a very sticky weed called goosegrass from the grassy banks, the goal being to aim its long green strands at the unsuspecting uncles' immaculate black serge backs, there to remain firmly stuck throughout the chapel service until discovered and removed. We were never told off about it, they seemed to take it as a matter of course – the sort of thing we did – it didn't bother them.

The fun was that we thought it was all secret, but retrospectively the uncles probably knew all the time, because they were so tolerant, and liked a bit of fun themselves. They were all simply lovely and played many a trick back on us when the opportunity presented itself. However, if tales were told to Mamgu then we had better look out, for she expected high and respectful standards of behaviour from man and beast, keeping her late husband's blackthorn stick handy at all times. She wasn't afraid to use it either, viz a relative who once staggered drunk into the yard and was beaten off the premises with no mercy, not to be seen ever again in that disgraceful state.

THE IRON ROLLER

This painting centres around a gigantic iron roller which had shafts for a horse. This was used to roll the tennis court in front of the farmhouse, a facility rented out to people from the town in the summer, so pre-summer there was always a furore getting the grass back into shape. After cutting, it was rollered flat by the horse-drawn roller. The horse was an old grey called Farmer. Poor horse, he was such a dear, good horse, but later had to be put down because the tendon or ligament under his tongue had been torn, probably by barbed wire somewhere, so that he couldn't eat or drink. Back to rollering the tennis court: the racket as the metal crashed over small boulders en route from the yard soon gave way to soft silence as Farmer was turned onto the grass. Meanwhile, we children followed, hopping, skipping and jumping, eventually fighting for positions on top of the vast roller, and off we'd go. It was a wonderful source of tricks and games and fun for us. We are all featured in the painting doing various acrobatics as Farmer pulled us along, guided by a very patient uncle. What is not portrayed is what could have been a serious accident when the smallest of us fell off and the roller actually went over his hand, arm and shoulder. We all screamed and shouted and the uncle reacted swiftly by bringing Farmer to an abrupt halt and hauling the child out.

We gasped in horror at what might have been as we all inspected the dent left in the, fortunately, soft ground. There was the imprint of his bent arm – his elbow, shoulder, hand – luckily, we had stopped at his chest. After completing the rollering out would come the liming gadgets, a square can on a stick, a small, wide wheel fixed to the front plus a bucket of lime ready to pour into the can. Immaculate lines were drawn on the lawn by one of the uncles after much measuring with an old, frayed cloth tape measure. Woe betide any child who stepped on the white lines before they had dried. The antidote to this crime was for us to rush down to the bottom field, there to hollow out bowers in the rapidly growing grass from where we whooped like wild things, shooting imaginary arrows and dropping down dead in imaginary agony.

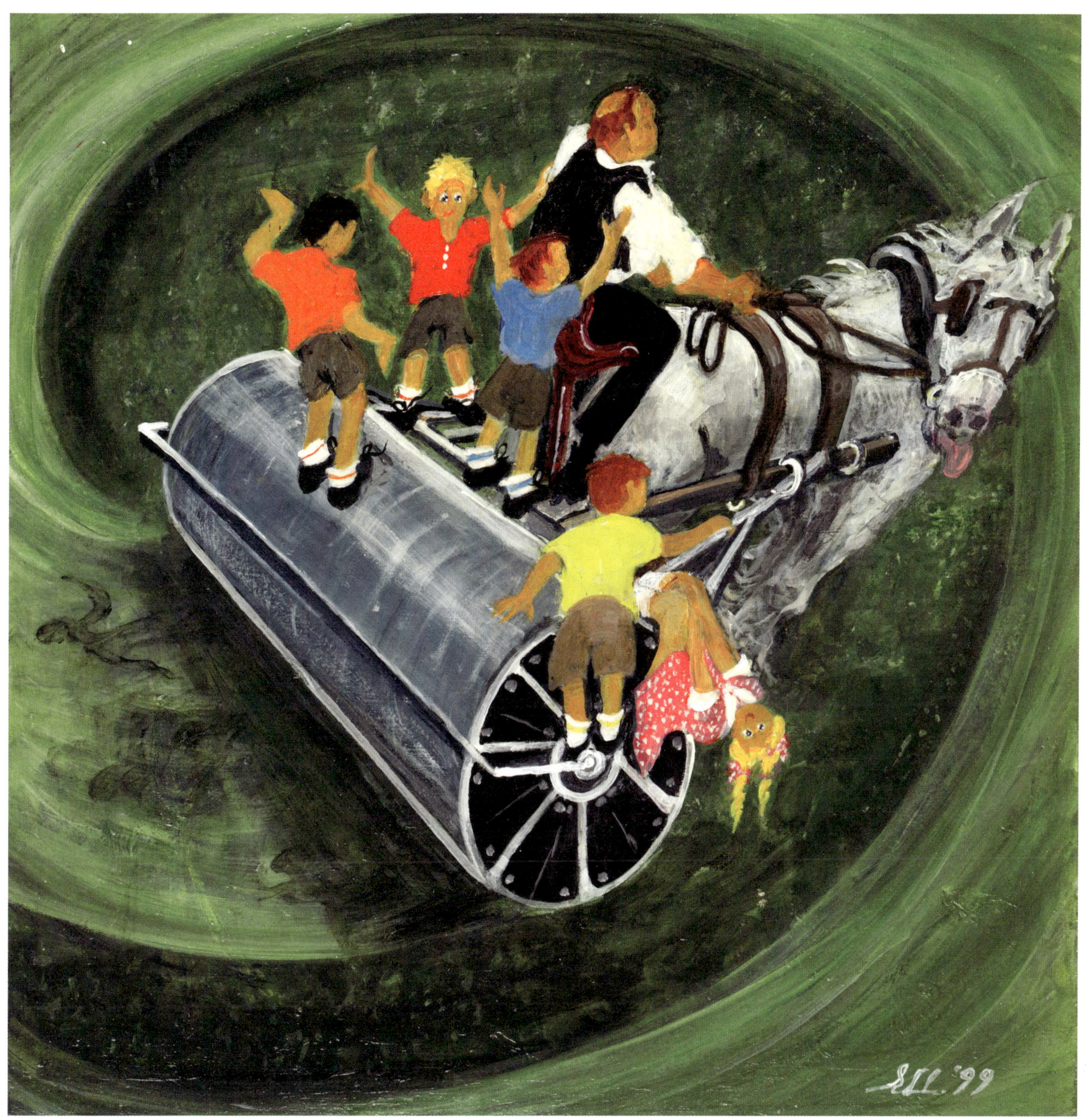

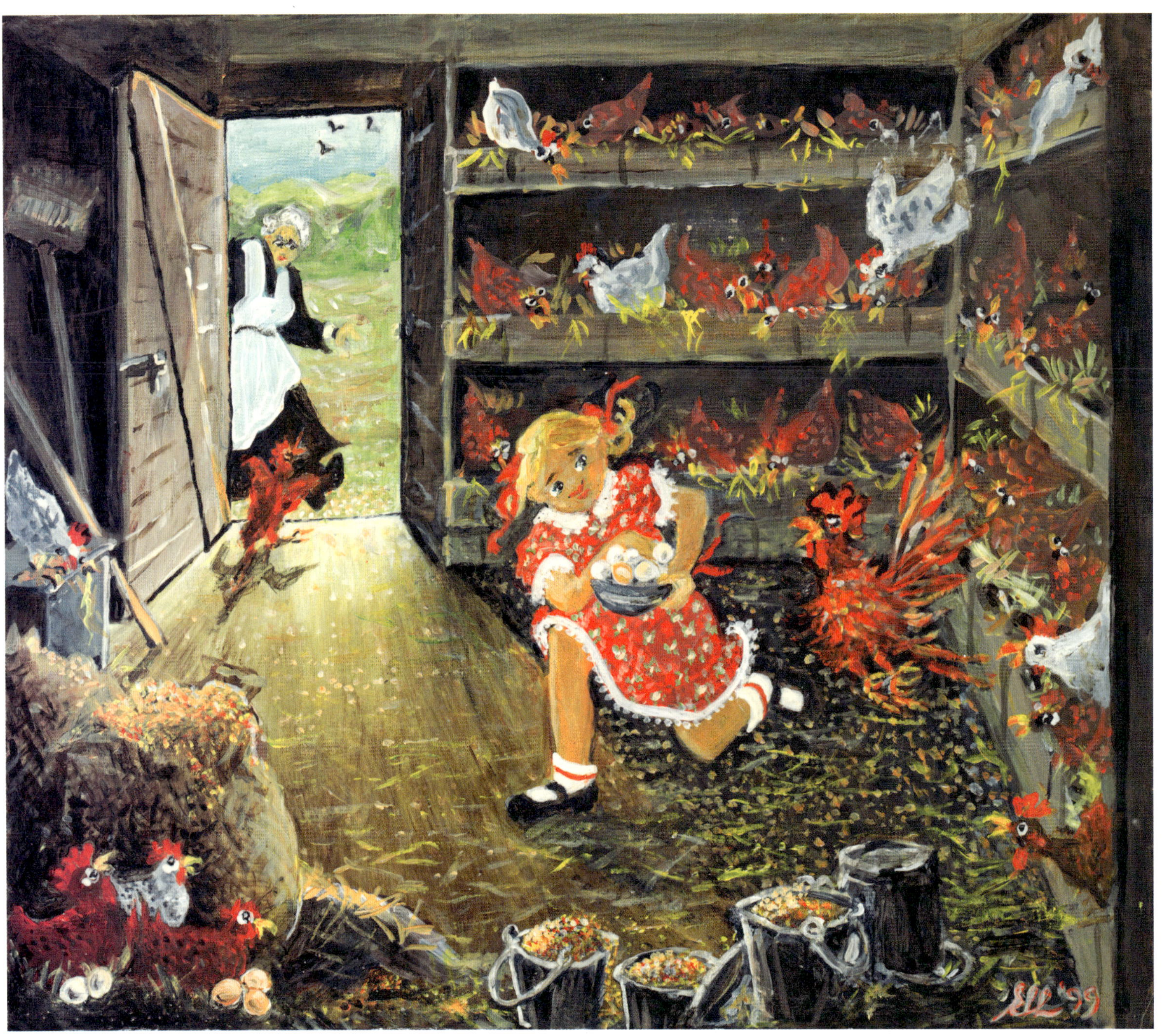

COLLECTING THE EGGS

This painting depicts the henhouse and the marvellous expedition I would go on, with great trepidation, upon Mamgu's instructions. With a wide metal bowl tucked under my arm, large enough to hold about three dozen newly laid eggs – white, cream, brown, speckled – I would definitely be running the gauntlet because the hens and cockerels, objected strongly by attacking me, and flying at me to get this intruder, this little girl, out of their henhouse, their citadel. I had to feel around in any empty nests; very often there would be nothing in this lovely warm bowl of yellow straw. At other times I'd have to squeeze my hand underneath a heavy, hot-feathered hen, if I could see eggs peeping out from under it, 'shoo' it away, quickly seize the eggs, very gently and carefully, then lower them gently into the metal bowl.

I would race off at top speed – it had to be a very fast exercise in case I got pecked to death or feathered to death or suffocated by a million motes in the sun-beamed air, tiny feathers blinding me and choking me. Sometimes Mamgu would hear the racket and come to see if I was alright, and were the hens alright? But the pride of having such marvellous treasures to carry back, such smooth and delicate objects, nature's nourishment for enterprising mankind, was overwhelming.

SCARECROW

This scene is about Mamgu's wonderful strawberry beds and their protection from greedy crows and even greedier children, both hell-bent upon stealing the precious fruit. The scarecrow is the real feature here – a structure of bits of wood, straw and a large swede with an uncle's old, worn-out coat and trousers, the whole thing tied together with cord before being stuck into a deep hole with stones and tamped in to make it secure. The strawberry crop came again and again in ever-increasing waves of sweet-sour succulence, their ripeness encouraged through all weathers by high but distant walls. Other fruit flourished there too, plums, greengages, apples, pears and cherries. Nobody ever noticed the gang raid on the strawberries, or else they didn't mind because of superabundance – whichever – the crime carried its own punishment in the form of acute stomachache that night and anguished howls of pain.

The garden in general was Mamgu's domain, with only a little help from a hired farm labourer seasonally. The garden was sacrosanct, a status invaded by a kid goat taken in from a school friend's family by myself on the false assurance that it would be safe on my grandmother's farm. Goats are notorious for snatching and gobbling anything edible or inedible, and thus suffer banishment from valuables of any kind. However, the garden door was carelessly left open one day and in the kid raced, soon demolishing every lettuce, bean, pea, raspberry and strawberry. Discovery led to rage from Mamgu and the kid disappeared, its fate a dark secret. I was in trouble for that. To return to the scarecrow – I was always fascinated by its face, eyes, nose and grinning mouth gouged out quite artistically by an uncle's penknife. The men always carried a penknife and a ball of twine, prerequisites for life on the land. The stomachache from the scarlet strawberries is so clear in my mind to this day that I turn away with a gulp every time I see one.

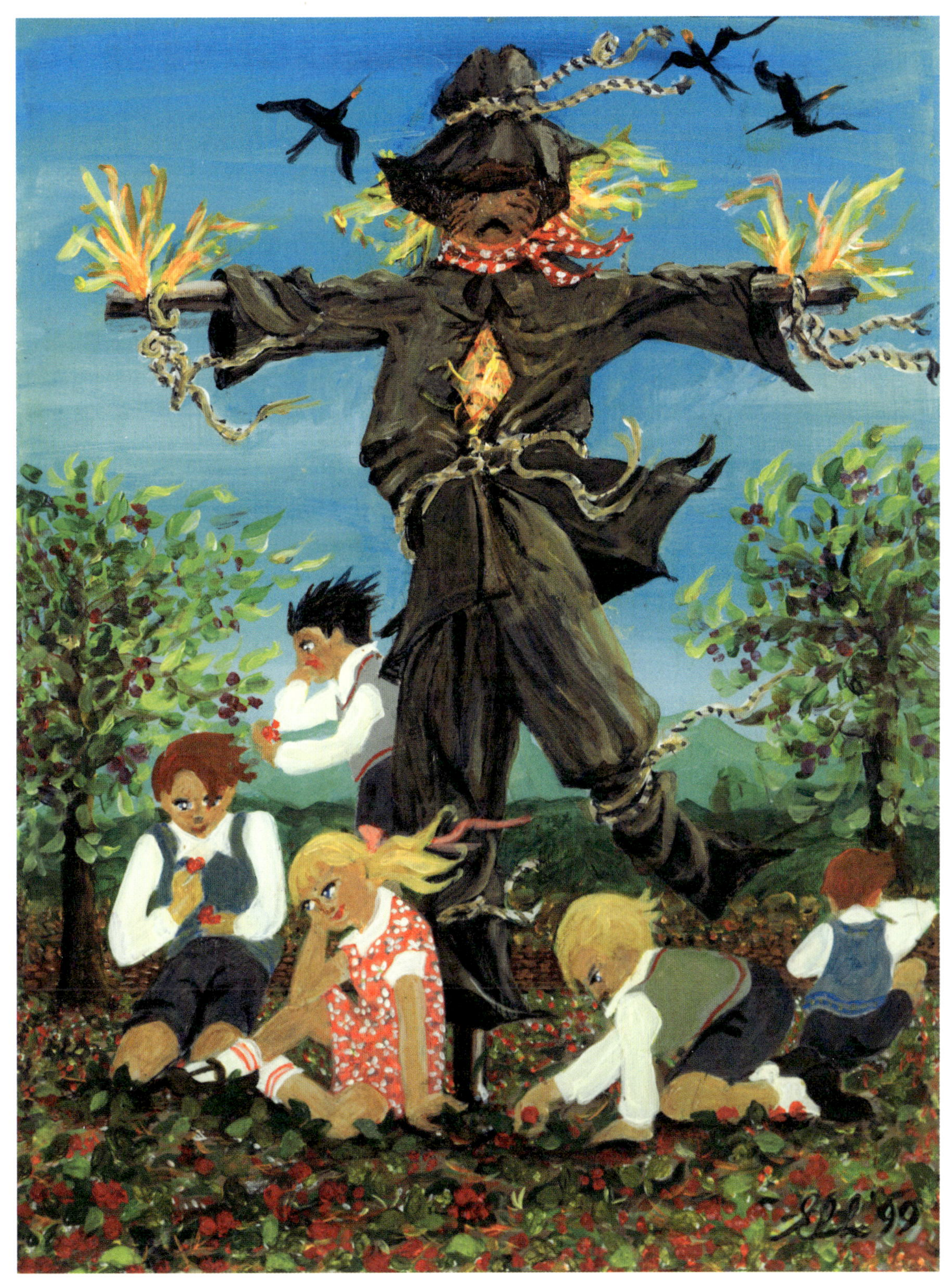

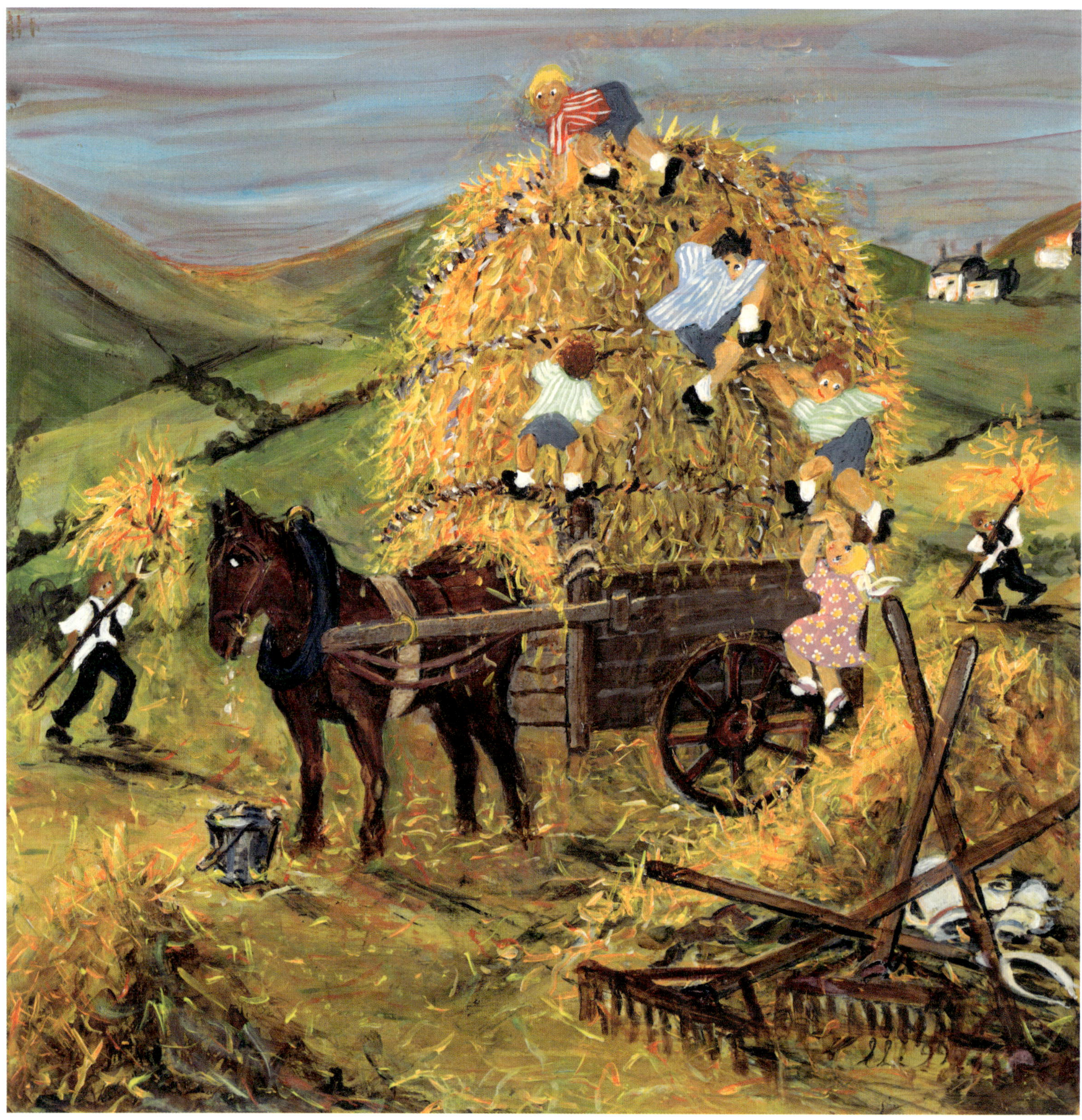

HAY HARVEST

This concerns haymaking in the month of August, and I so well remember setting off from the farmyard, sitting on the pine end of the empty gambo, feet dangling in the breeze as the wooden vehicle festooned with ropes on four posts and Captain, a dark bay old horse, pulling with all the might of his well-fed one horsepower. No fast car today can compete with the thrill of being towed along in the open air, hair flying in the wind, knuckles white from clinging on, as the gambo hit submerged boulders and sent us cousins bouncing into the air to crash down again with bone-bruising thuds.

Of course, we all had to squeeze onto the pine end. It was more risky there and there was more chance for the boys to pinch and thump each other en route to a distant golden field of sun-dried cut hay, all waiting to be raked up and transported home to the big barn and storage for the winter animal feed and bedding. Side to side the gambo would sway – bang! Crash! Captain's snorting and the creak of the leather harness combining with the jingle of brass ornaments raising the level of excitement, the scent of the hot horse hair and sweat enriching the perfume of grasses and flowered hedgerows until we finally slowed to turn in to our target. Sometimes we were there as the grass was being cut, the men using villainous long sharp

scythes, we children banished to sit on the gate or play hotly in the next field. As the tall grass fell, a small square was left uncut, and then the uncles would get out their guns, for into that square had run the rabbits, lots of them. We would sit on the gate under firm instruction not to move one inch. I always turned my head at this point and covered my ears with my hands, but nothing could shut out the cruel *'Bang! Bang! Bang! Bang!'* as the men shot off their guns. Then in they would go, emerging with little furry bodies dangling, held by their back legs. That was such a sad scene, and the rabbits would all be laid down in the shade of a hedge in little rows. I never did look at those except when it couldn't be helped. However, men must be fed, and Mamgu made a good rabbit stew, as well as selling on down at the market. The yellow scented hay was by then raked into pyramids five feet tall, into which we cousins dived playing hide-and-seek until midday when the men threw themselves and their rakes down to the ground and we children were ordered to go back to the farm for refreshments, thus earning our bread and butter, pulling our weight, good lessons learned early in life.

COLLECTING SAND

Another expedition full of thrills involved the replenishment of sand for Mamgu's kitchen floor. Scrubbing the floor daily was asking too much, so Gu's method was to sprinkle clean, fresh sand on the flagstones and then sweep the whole lot out, debris and all, last thing every night. Generous handfuls of new sand were then thrown down ready for the next day's onslaught, the flagstones thus purified and smelling of the sea. The source of the sand was sand dunes on the semi-industrial coastline several miles away. By this time Gu had acquired a brand-new Ford 8, gleamingly black with green leather upholstery, a marvellous thing at that time. Its numberplate was BNY 750. We descended upon BNY 750 like bees to a honeypot, five cousins squeezed into the back of a small two-doored car, fighting and elbowing each other in the race for seats by the windows. Most of the exciting expeditions took place during our school holidays. As with children everywhere, there was a competition as to who would be first to see the sea, and there would be plenty of cheating until the golden peaks of fine, sparkling sand rose into view, seemingly towering against the sky like Mt. Everest and the uncles changed gear to bottom, ready for the shock of sinking deep into swirled sand scattered with reeds, thus grinding to an abrupt halt.

The uncles did their usual teasing of us by continuing to sit in their seats so that we couldn't get out, it being a two-door car, until at last we were released like jacks-in-the-box, falling flat on our faces in a heap of flailing arms and legs and assorted yelps of complaint. The uncles quickly got down to business, unloaded the gear and began shovelling, one holding a sack open while the other shovelled sand in, taking it in turns, for it is hard work. In no time at all we had climbed a dune, skidding and sliding backwards, a mammoth effort, until we got to the beautiful top and came down again, whooping like a war party and scaring seagulls away from their peaceful domain. Most of all, it was the sense of liberation experienced which made the children so joyful and oh so reluctant to squeeze back into the sardine tin of everyday life, let alone BNY 750.

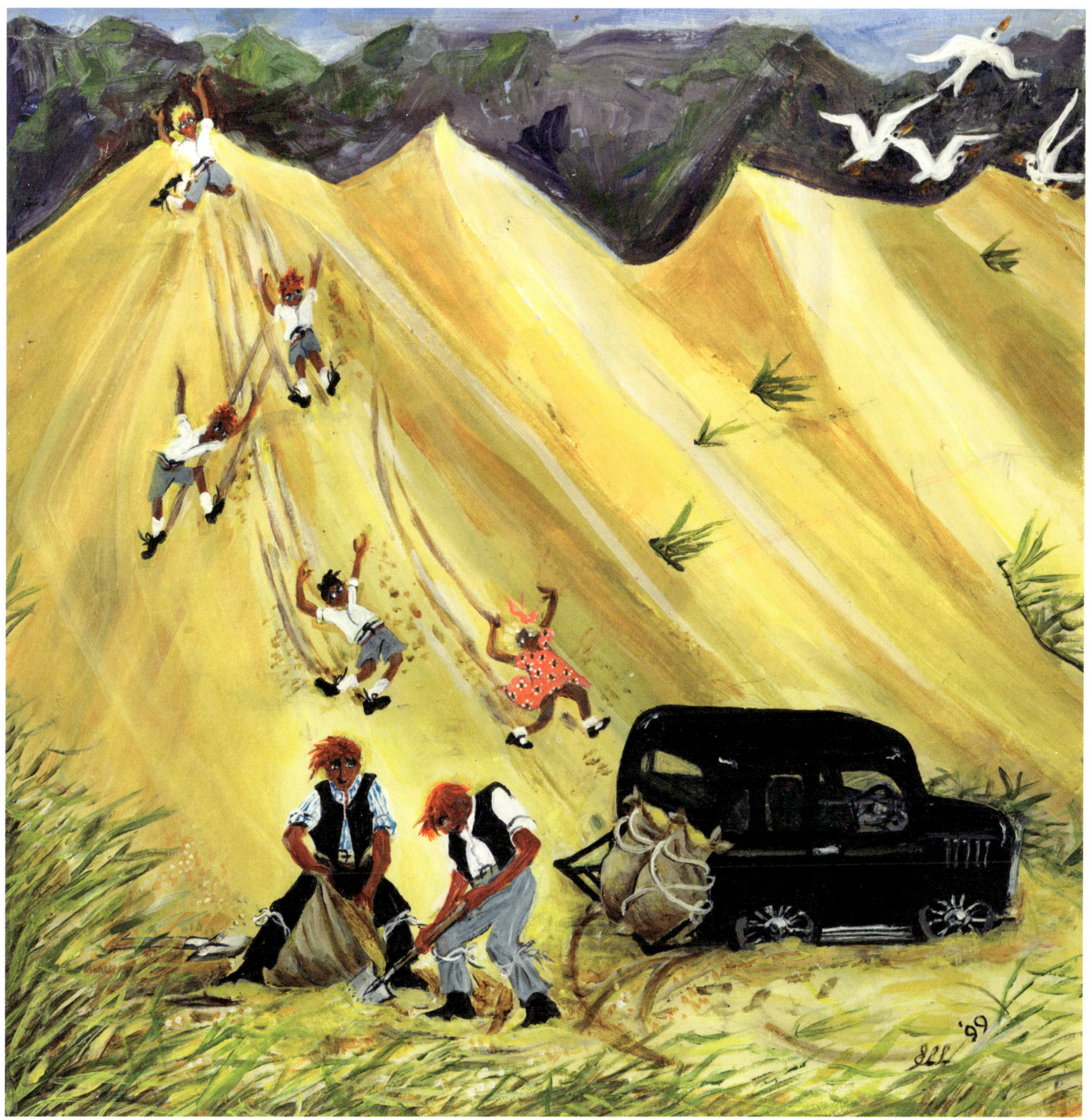

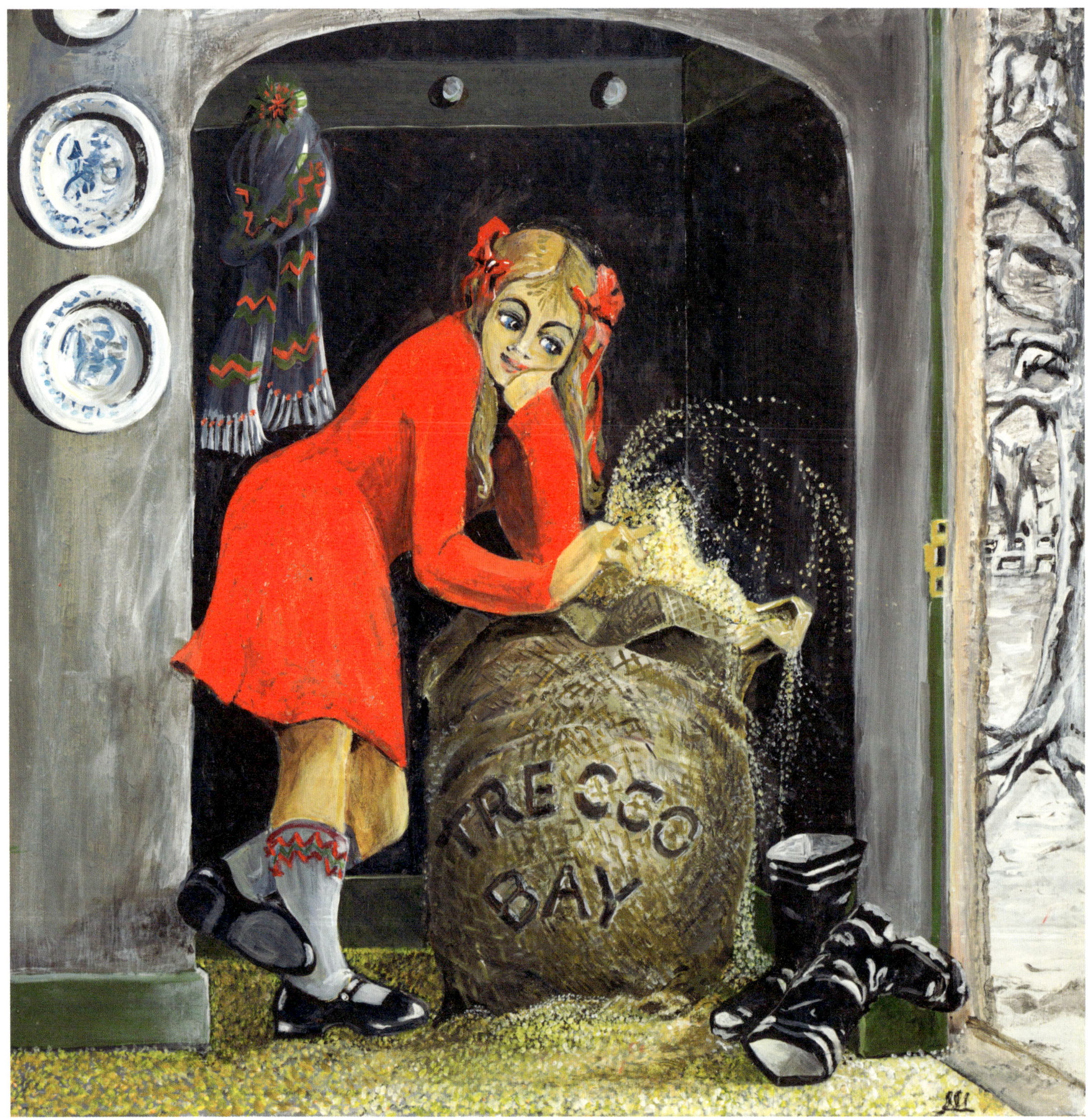

TRE CCO
BAY

REMEMBERING SUMMER

Painted a couple of years before the others, this was my first painting, which led me oh so slowly on the road of turning out over fifty in the years ahead. It must have been a cold, rainy day which drove me to this idea, because as I stared out at the wet roofs opposite and grey skies overhead, my memory leapt back to the scene here in this painting. I am in Mamgu's kitchen, leaning on the sack of sand collected from the dunes in previous months. It is midwinter. Christmas is over, there is nothing much to do and the world outside is depressingly monochrome. Thus, I decide to shrink myself down, in my imagination, to make miniature sand dunes up which I run to jump off the top like a seagull, arms outstretched, longing, as I have all my life, for the summer warmth and light to come back. It felt like a fruitless mental exercise because it had the effect of only making the prospect ahead worse.

FEEDING THE PIGS

This is a scene from when I was a little bit younger, helping Mamgu to feed the pigs, a cold, muddy exercise. This was terrifying due to the ferocity of the hungry, tetchy sows, whose litters of greedy piglets plagued them constantly. Mamgu was not a person with whom a child could have any fun, quite the reverse, but you could gain some meagre sort of acceptance by being helpful, so, somehow I would find myself entering the long, low building which housed all the animal feed, plus a coal-fired brazier for boiling up and sterilising the pigswill. All around were bulging sacks of delicious looking 'nuts' of compacted feed which looked just like toffees, so that if you tried one because it looked so enticing, you'd get a very nasty shock indeed. It tasted absolutely revolting, so it had to be spat out quickly, your greedy little idea soon demolished. But for the pigs, my goodness, it was a marvellous feast. So here we are now, Gu and myself, placing a bucket of peelings from every fruit and vegetable available – but never greens, for they would scour the pigs intestines, even kill them – placing the bucket on the now burning brazier.

A handful of 'nuts' thrown in, and plenty of stirring with an ancient bleached stick, cut from somewhere, soon produced a mouthwatering aroma which drifted over to the pigsties, driving the occupants into an even worse frenzy. Finally, everything cooked to Gu's satisfaction, off we would go across the slippery yard, sharing the handle, hot though it was, and taking care not to spill any or scald ourselves. Once outside the heavy door, Gu hitched up her skirts, straightened her battered black felt hat, its silver hatpin standing aloft like a mast – her signal – then in she barged, slamming the low gate behind her to disappear, swearing in Welsh, into the thick of it, emerging later in a very dishevelled state, me white as a sheet from fear for her. Once back in the warm refuge of the kitchen I would beg the usual treat – a freshly cut crust of home-baked bread spread thick with homemade butter. My *'Diolch, Gu!'* fell on deaf ears, so off I went to play again. I didn't mind, I understood.

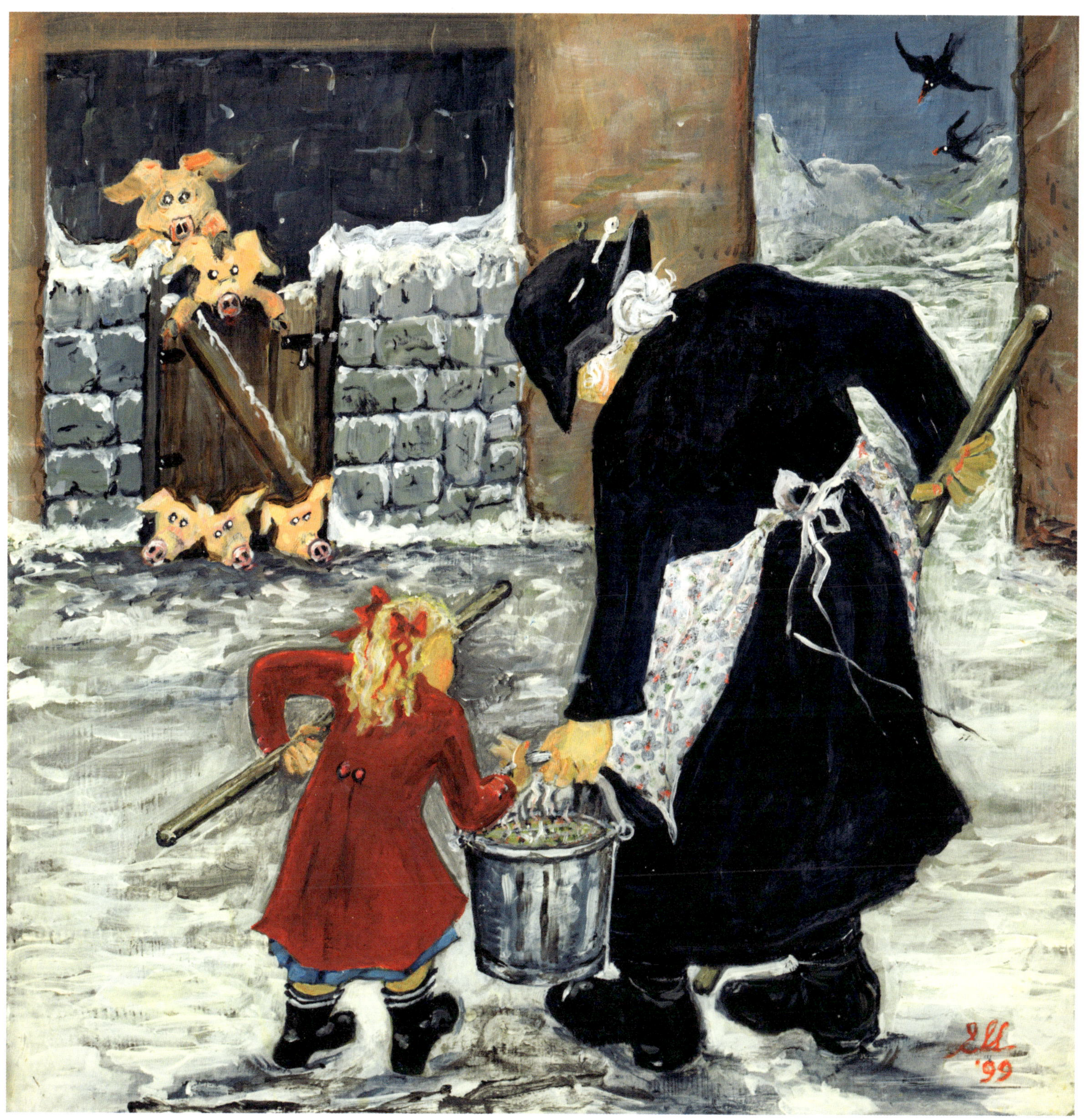

HOLIDAY

The acquisition by my father of our Ford 8, registration number CNY 616, black with red leather upholstery, robbed us of the sociability of public transport but compensated by introducing new adventures. The trip from Mamgu's farm presented an open invitation from one driver to another to enter into a reckless race. Because there were so few cars about at that time, drivers could, with a nod and a wink, challenge each other to prove who was the best driver. The hazards presented by the wild terrain of that area are legend now. In our case the car was packed to the roof, my brother and I squeezed into the last six inches sideways on our stomachs. Atop the roof was my father's old student-days trunk, bulging like an overfed elephant – my mother was merciless in the amount of things she packed. My father only ever lost one race, and that was because my mother screamed so much, she having chosen as her spouse a man who was still at heart a wild, rugby-playing, beer-drinking student, not a wise choice for her, being a tiny, delicate young woman of a nervous disposition.

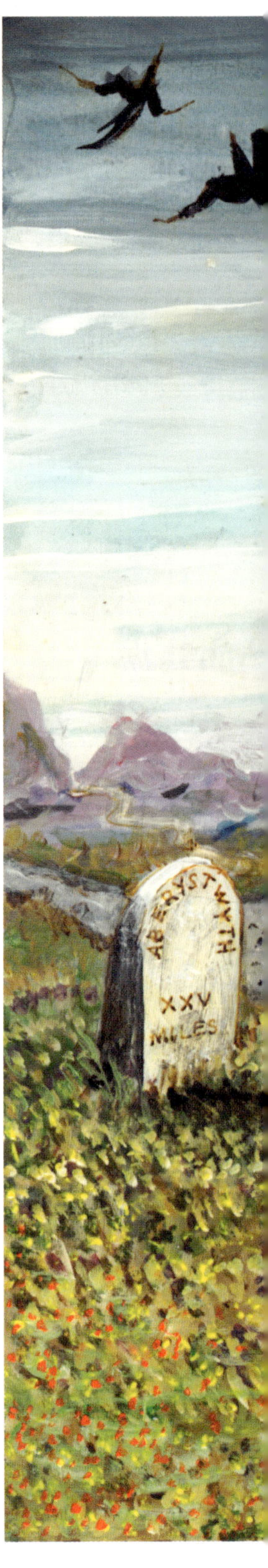

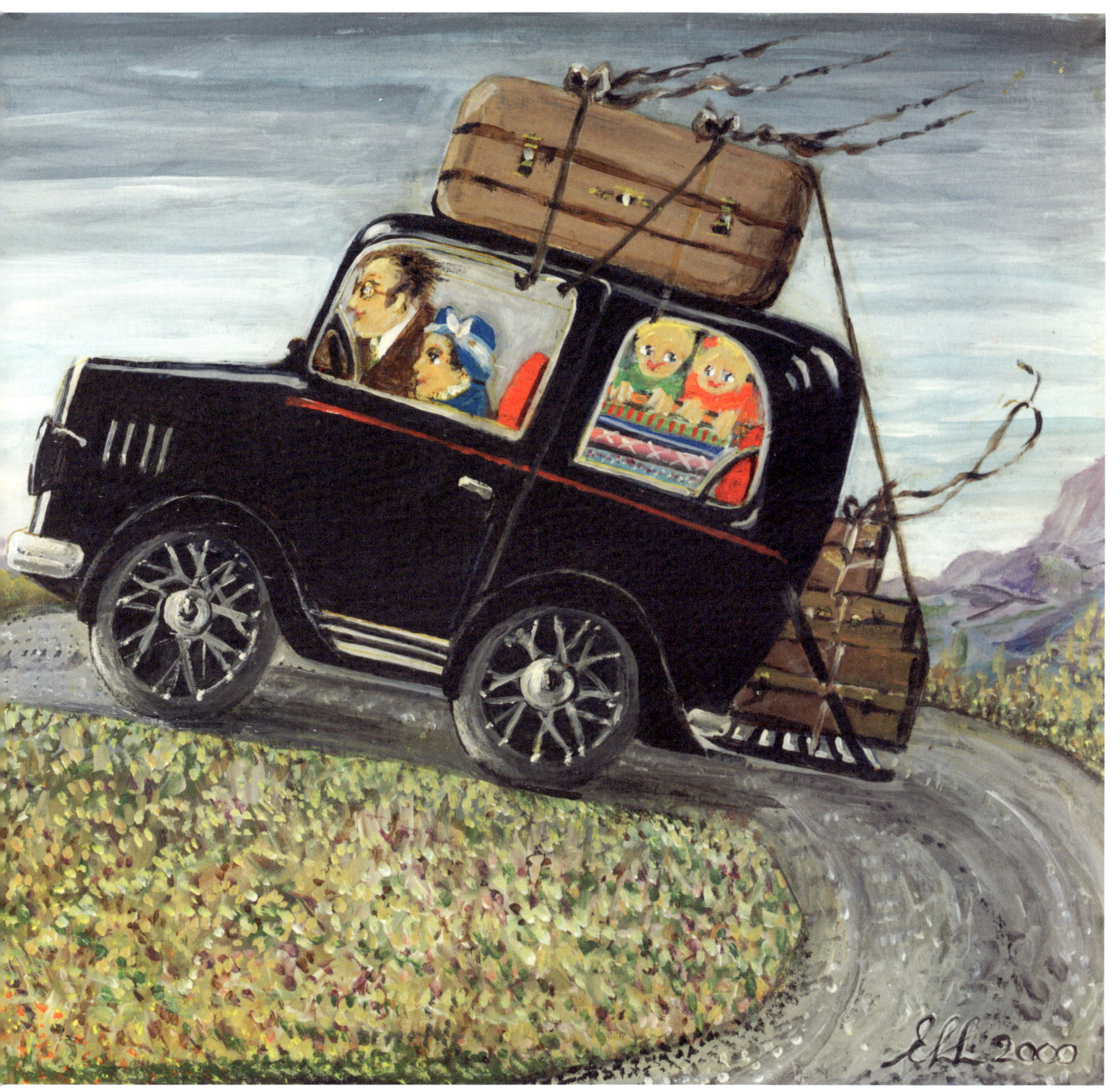

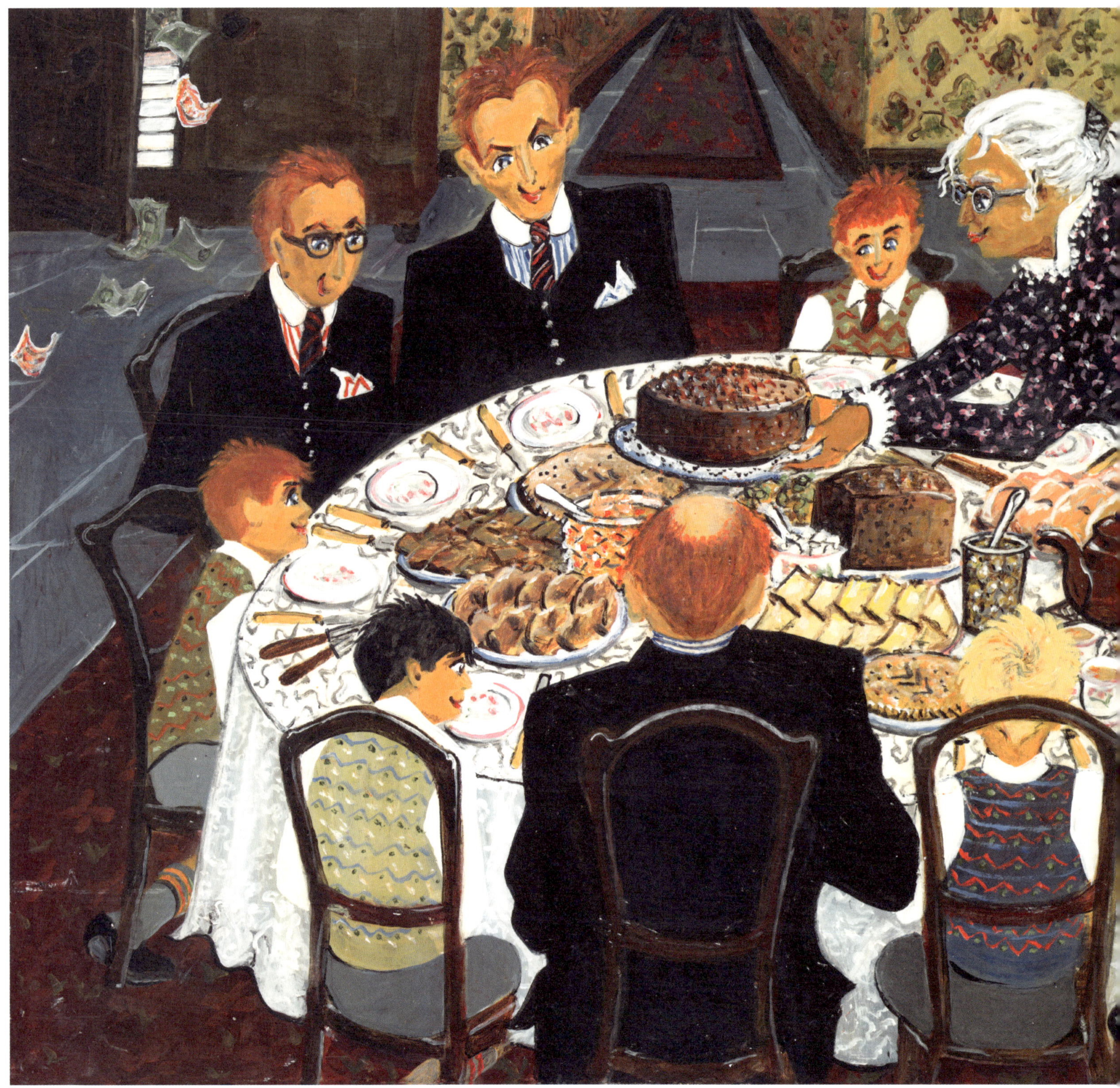

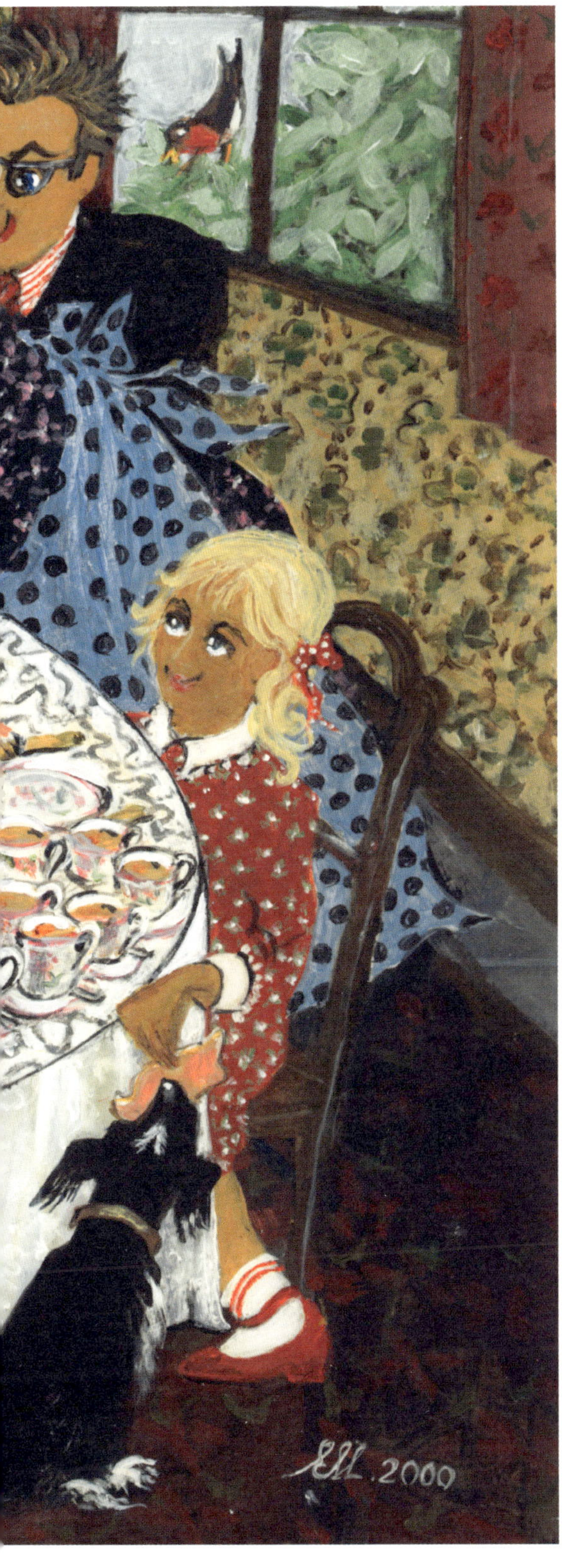

SUNDAY TEA

This painting demonstrates the bounty of Sunday tea at Mamgu's. I note that it is remarkable for the paucity of women present, Gu and I being the only females. The rest were uncles, cousins, my father and brother, the reason being bachelorhood, widowhood or illness. Everyone would be in their best Sunday clothes to properly mark their day of rest. A few painting corrections leap at me, for example the colour of the fruit tart pastry tops shouldn't be golden brown but white, speckled with fine black soot from the inside of the cast-iron coal-fired oven. Strangely, the flavour of shortcrust pastry made with flour and lard wasn't affected, providing delicious support to fruits from the farm – gooseberries, redcurrants, blackcurrants, apples and sometimes blackberries from wild hedgerows. We also had tinned peaches, considered a luxury, plus tinned cream, likewise very posh. Human beings are very funny, today it's the other way round and a certain superiority lies in home-produced food.

SUNDAY SCHOOL

So, did I really know why I went to church? The answer is 'yes', because as an infant-school pupil at a church school, I stumbled across the church's Children's Corner during playtime and instantly fell under the spell of all the stories of Jesus, avidly reading about him, lingering there, unable to tear myself away. That gift of discovery has never left me; I feel blessed for that.

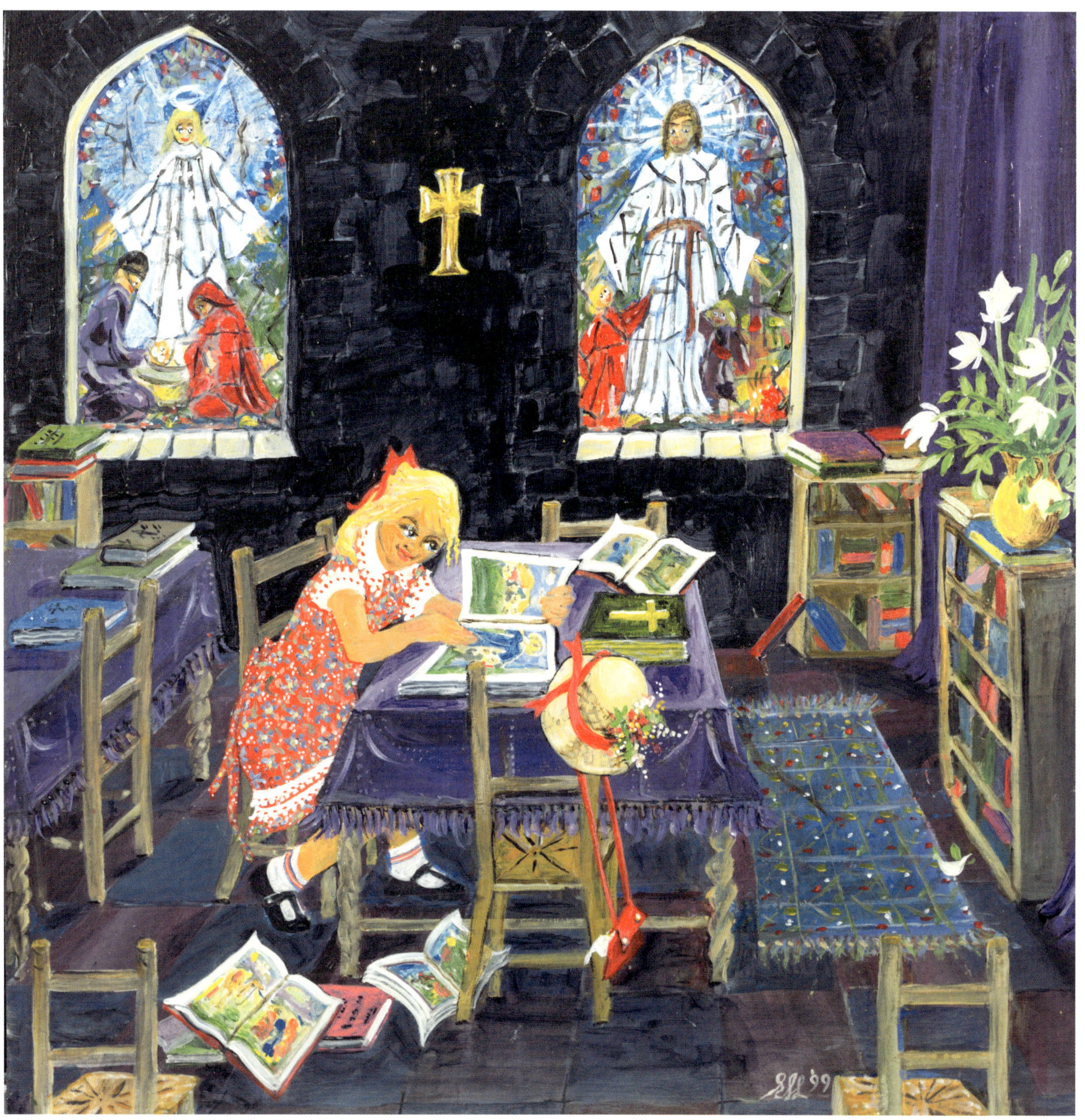

WASHDAY

Back down to earth, it's Monday – washday – on Mamgu's farm, where I grew up, and white sheets and other things have to be boiled in the coal-fired copper boiler located in the small wash-house in the small yard, under the trees. Everything is white, white, white. My grandmother, small but strong, is rubbing dirty clothes on a brass rubbing board, the friction of its ridges loosening dirt but at the same time rubbing fingers sore, a painful outcome experienced by myself when helping my mother for years. For drying, a rope clothesline was raised sky-high by a prop made from a long branch with a notch cut in the top. The wooden pegs we used were from travellers who passed through often and sold them door to door. Ironing was done by a heavy cast-iron iron heated over hot coals or gas flame if lucky, a thick cloth on the handle preventing burns. I remember how lovely it was sleeping on sheets dried in the fresh air.

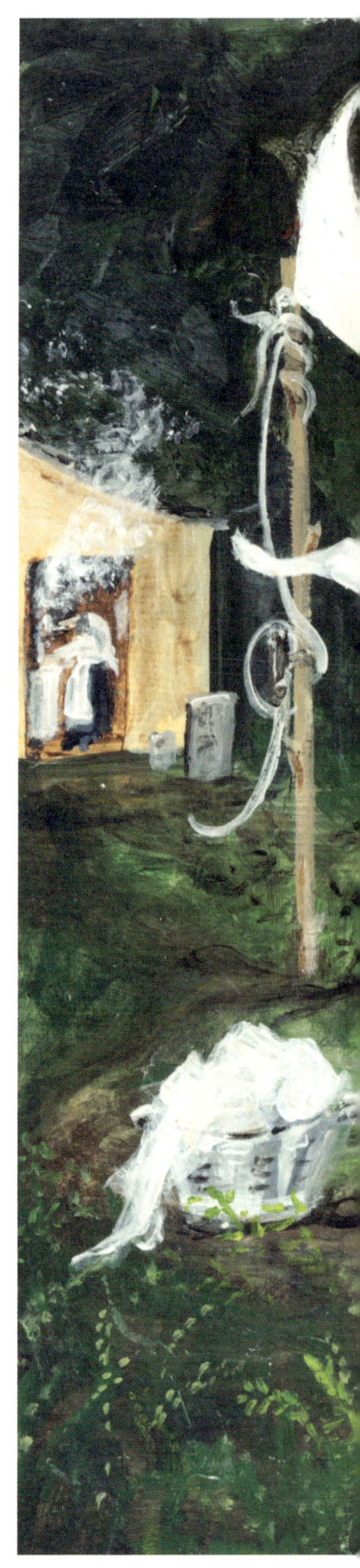

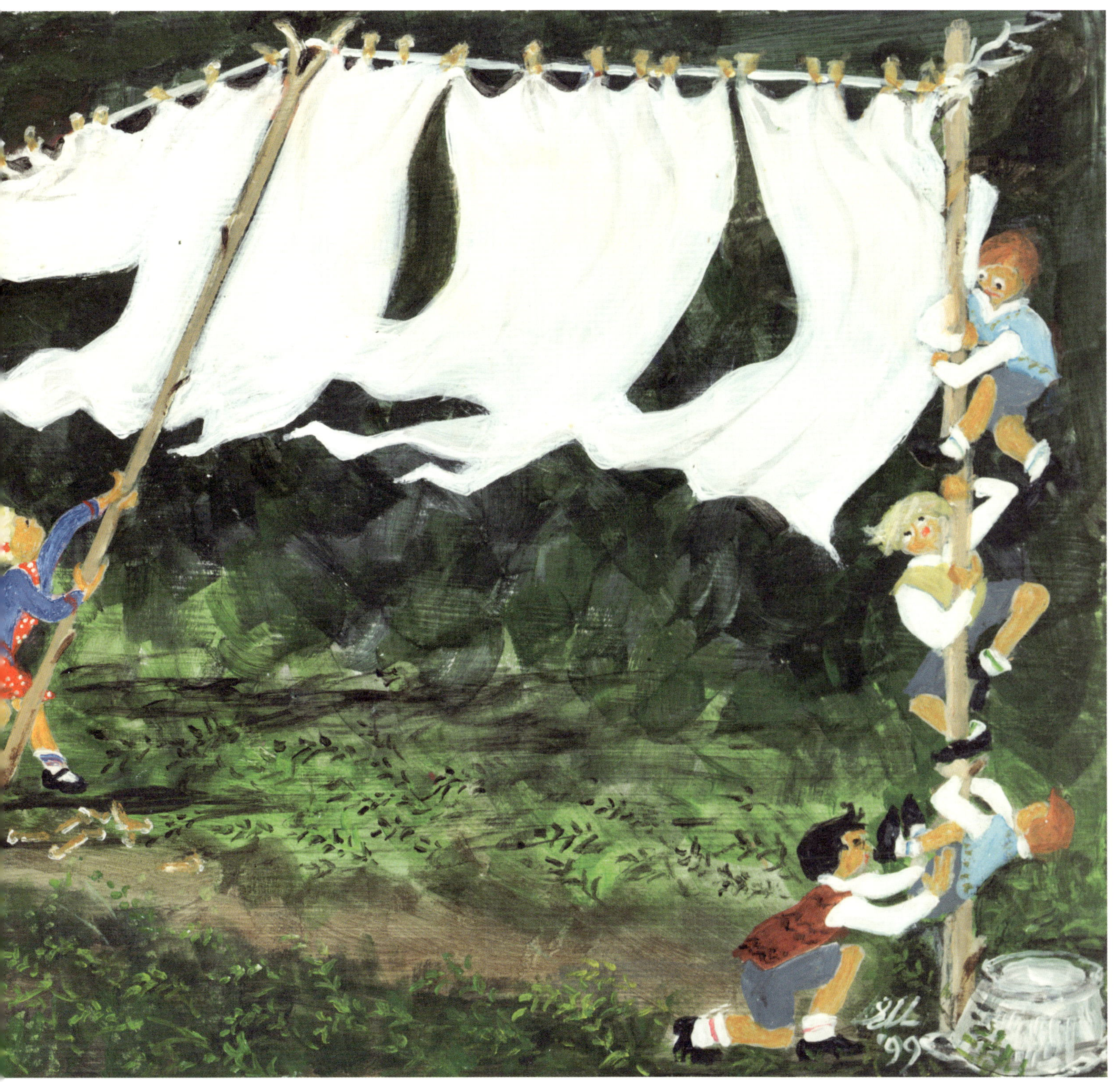

POTATO FIELD

This is Mamgu out in the potato fields, doing the work of two men as usual. Everything but horse-drawn ploughing had to be done by hand, including the planting and the picking, in all weathers, and she is carrying home two small sacks for immediate personal use. Her only protection from wind and rain is sacking tied around her shoulders and another round her middle to protect her clothes. Astonishingly, Gu was always immaculately clean, having her own bathroom upstairs in the farmhouse. However, I have the memory of her at the end of each day (except Sundays) stripping off to her waist in the kitchen despite the general melee of men and grandchildren.

We little ones would look on in awe as she took a flannel, dipping it in hot water boiled in the kettle over the coal fire, and a bar of household soap – nothing scented and lovely, of course. Then she would wash: arms, neck, underarms, face, ears and as far as she could reach around her back. She reminded me of a bumble-bee working away at pollen in flowers – slow, steady, with good staying power. I admired this small powerhouse of a woman, harsh though her attitude generally was – a lonely figure really, as befits all leaders, I suppose, for she was certainly that.

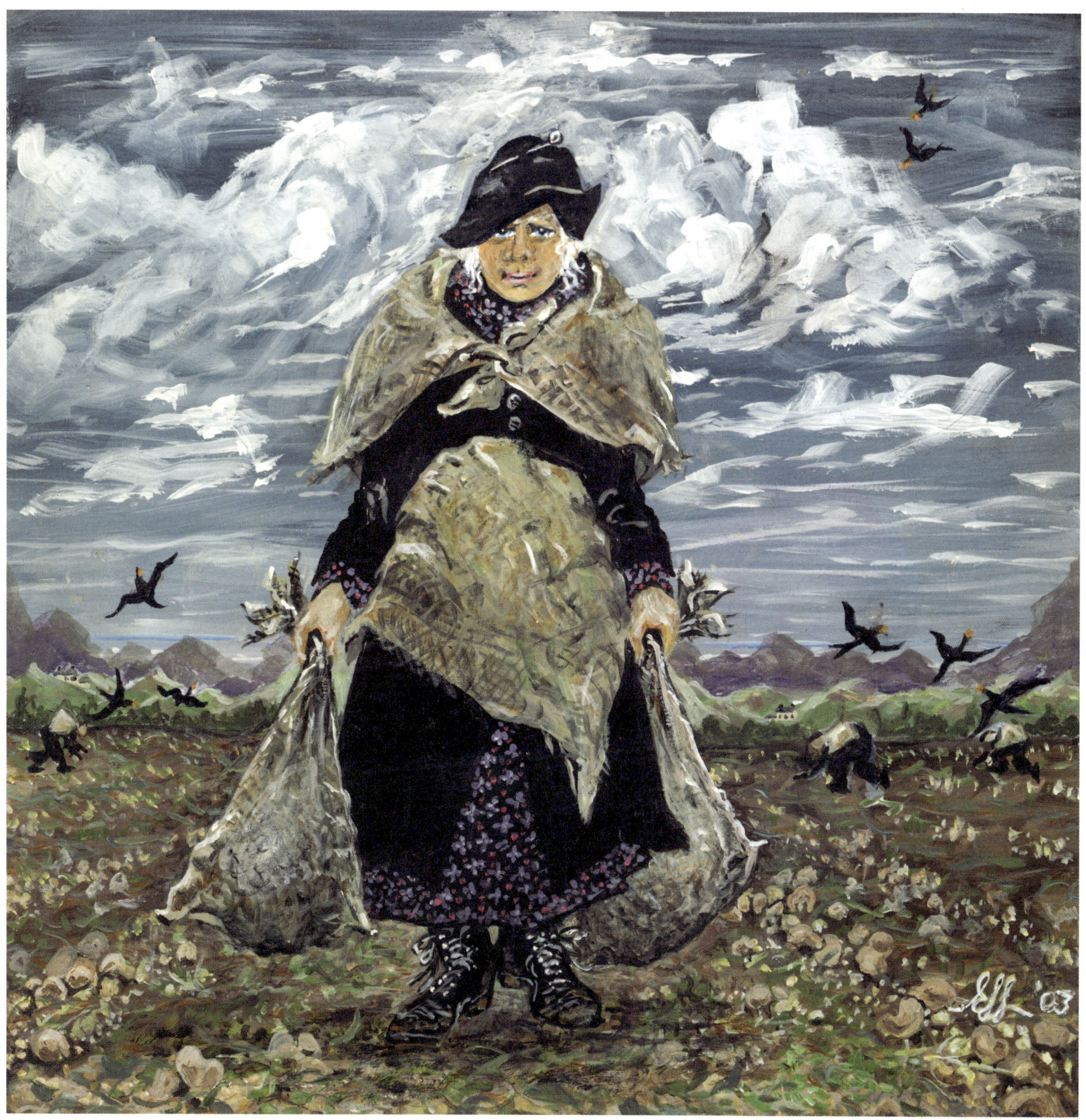

MILKING

I was fascinated by the procedure for milking the cows, though I never actually laid hands on an udder myself because the cows had a nasty habit of kicking when in the mood – I saw my grandmother Gu fly off her stool onto the floor many times. My job was to take each full pail of milk across the yard to the dairy. When you went in there you had the lovely scent of cleanliness. How they managed to keep it so hygienic in its cleanliness, I don't know – it smelt utterly, purely clean. In the centre stood some sort of structure which ran in tiers like a wedding cake, I thought. Icy-cold clean water spurted out of the top like a fountain, running down the sides and tiers, chilling the sterilised metal jugs into which the milk was carefully poured from the pail of warm milk straight from the cow. From there it was poured into metal milkchurns with tight lids. In no time at all it would be on the back of the horse-drawn milk cart on its way to delivery door to door.

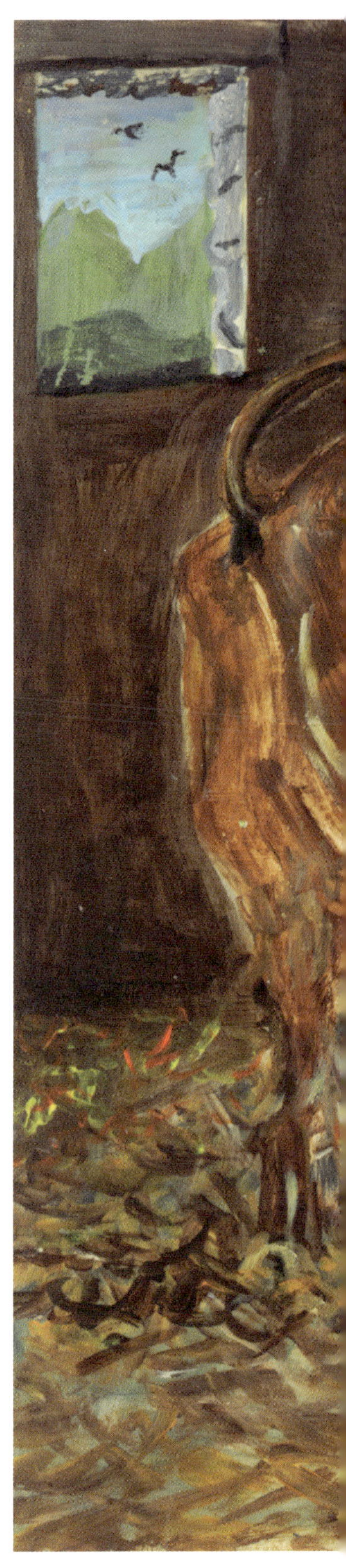

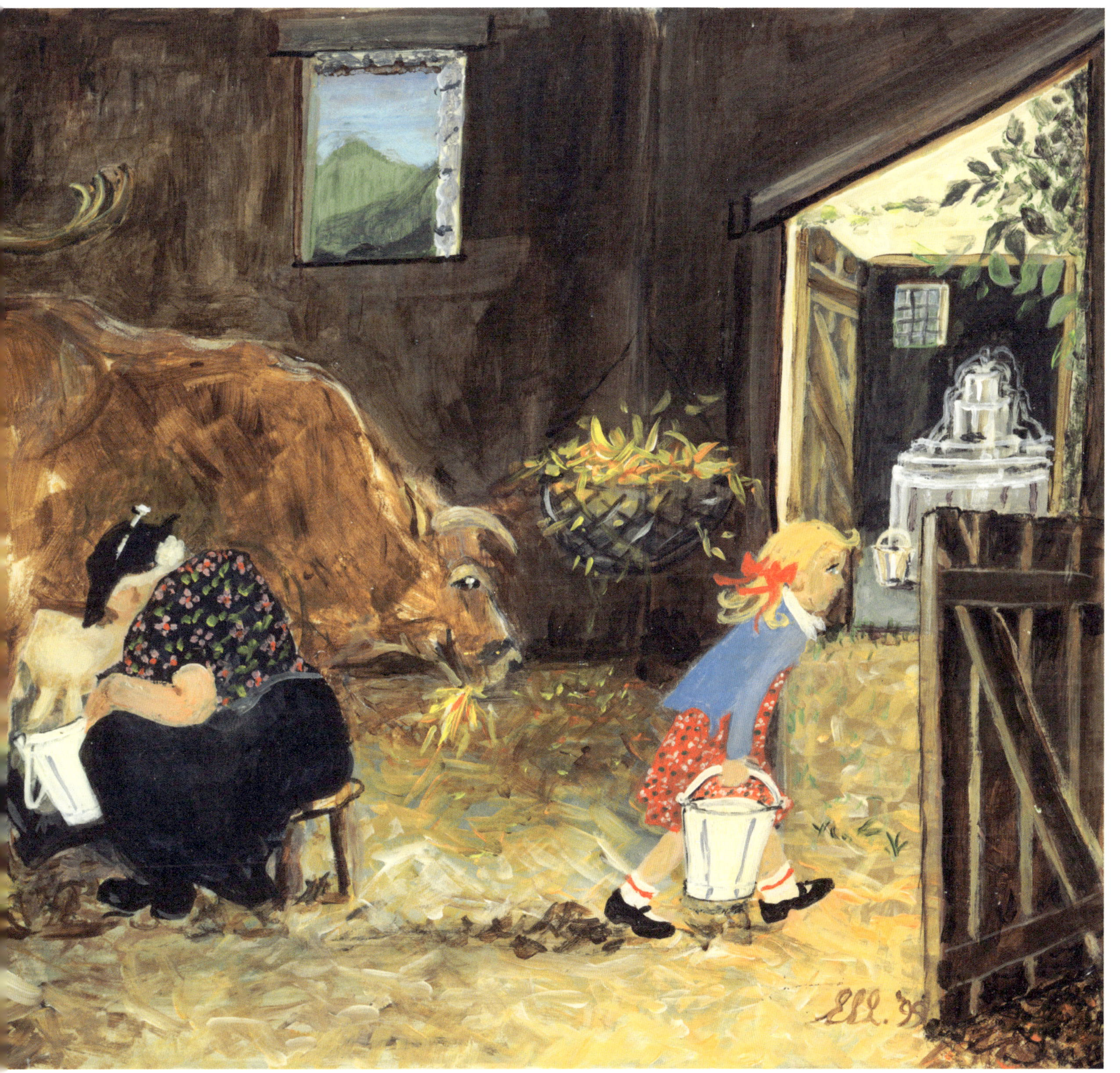

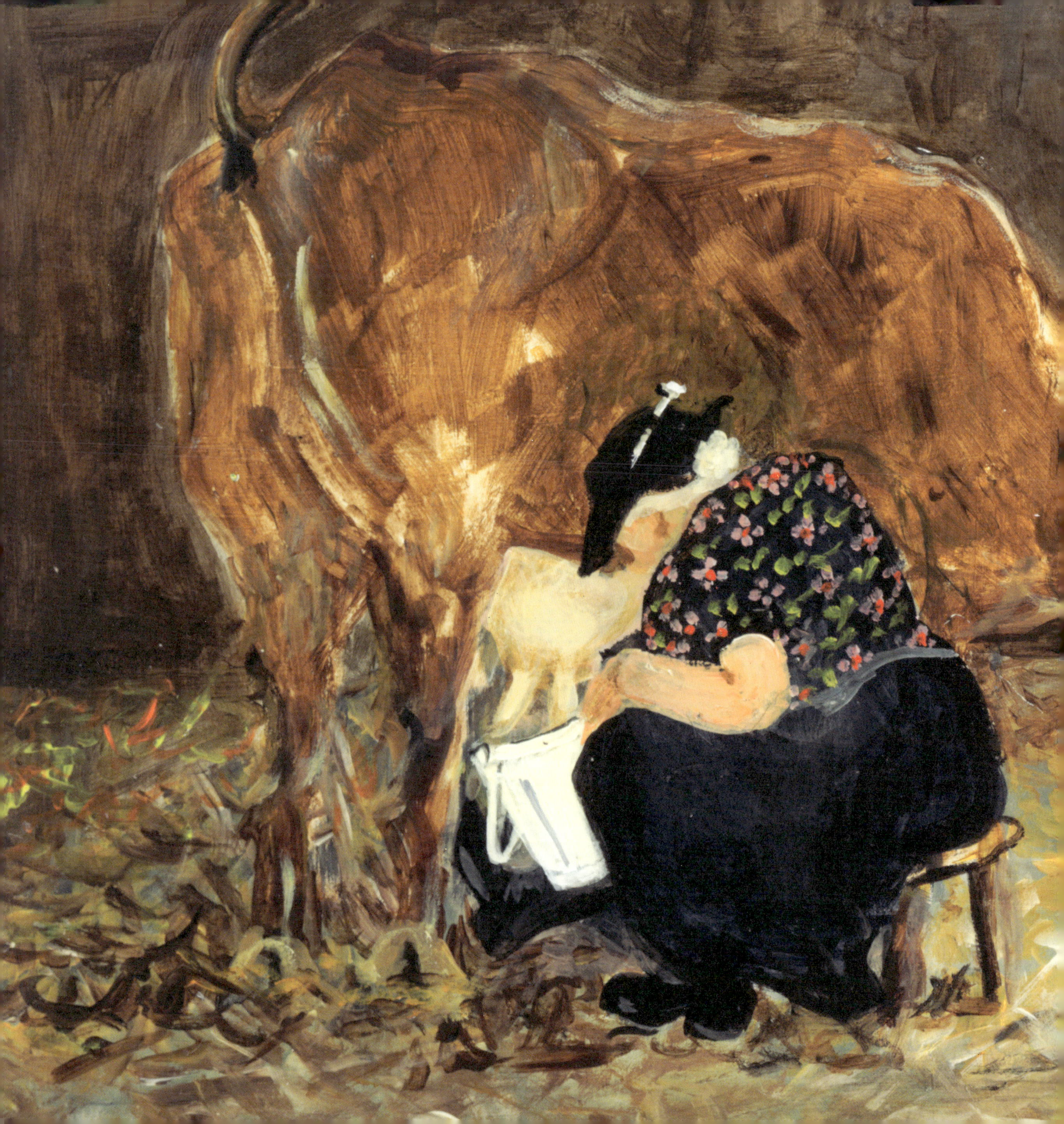

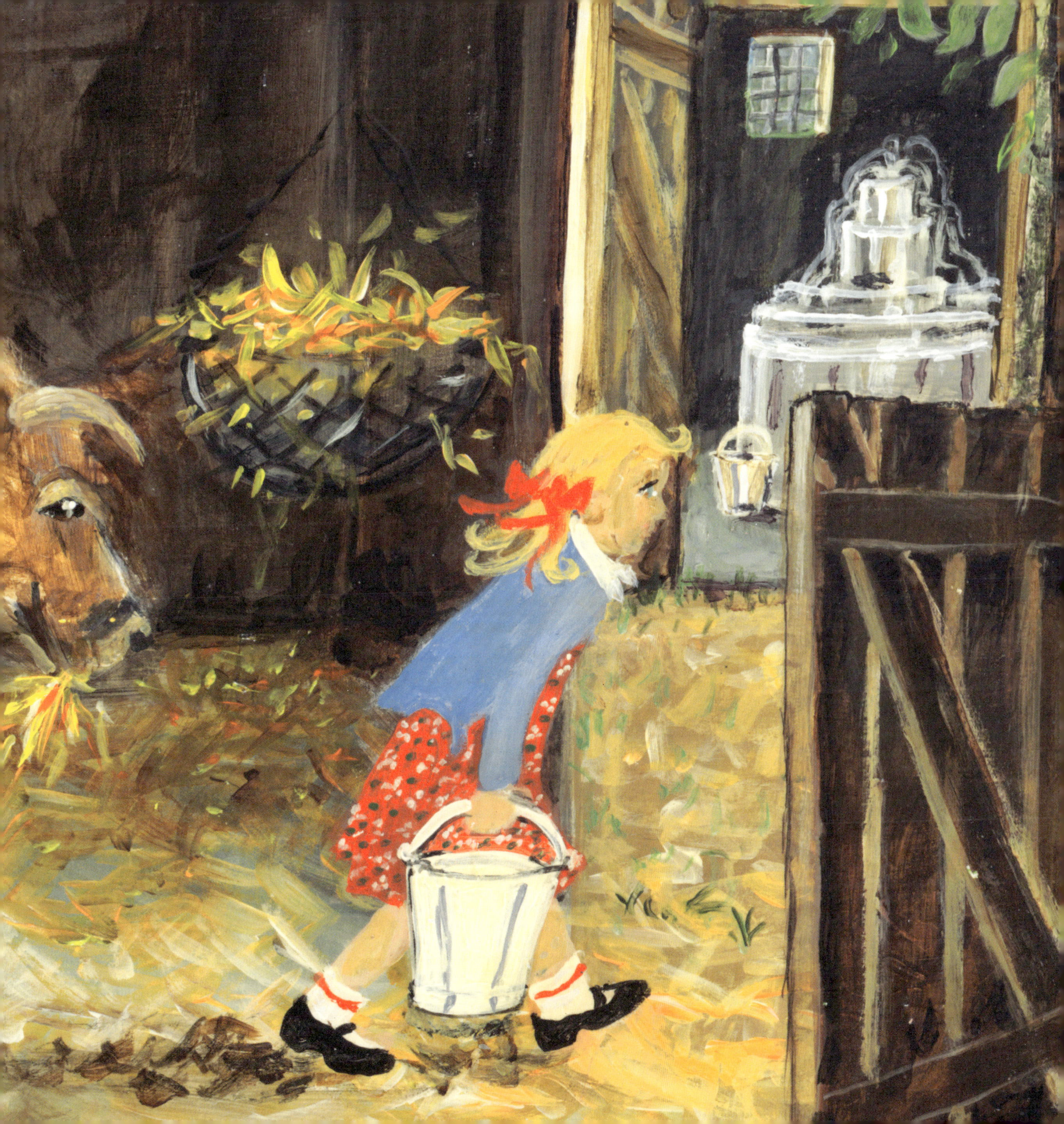

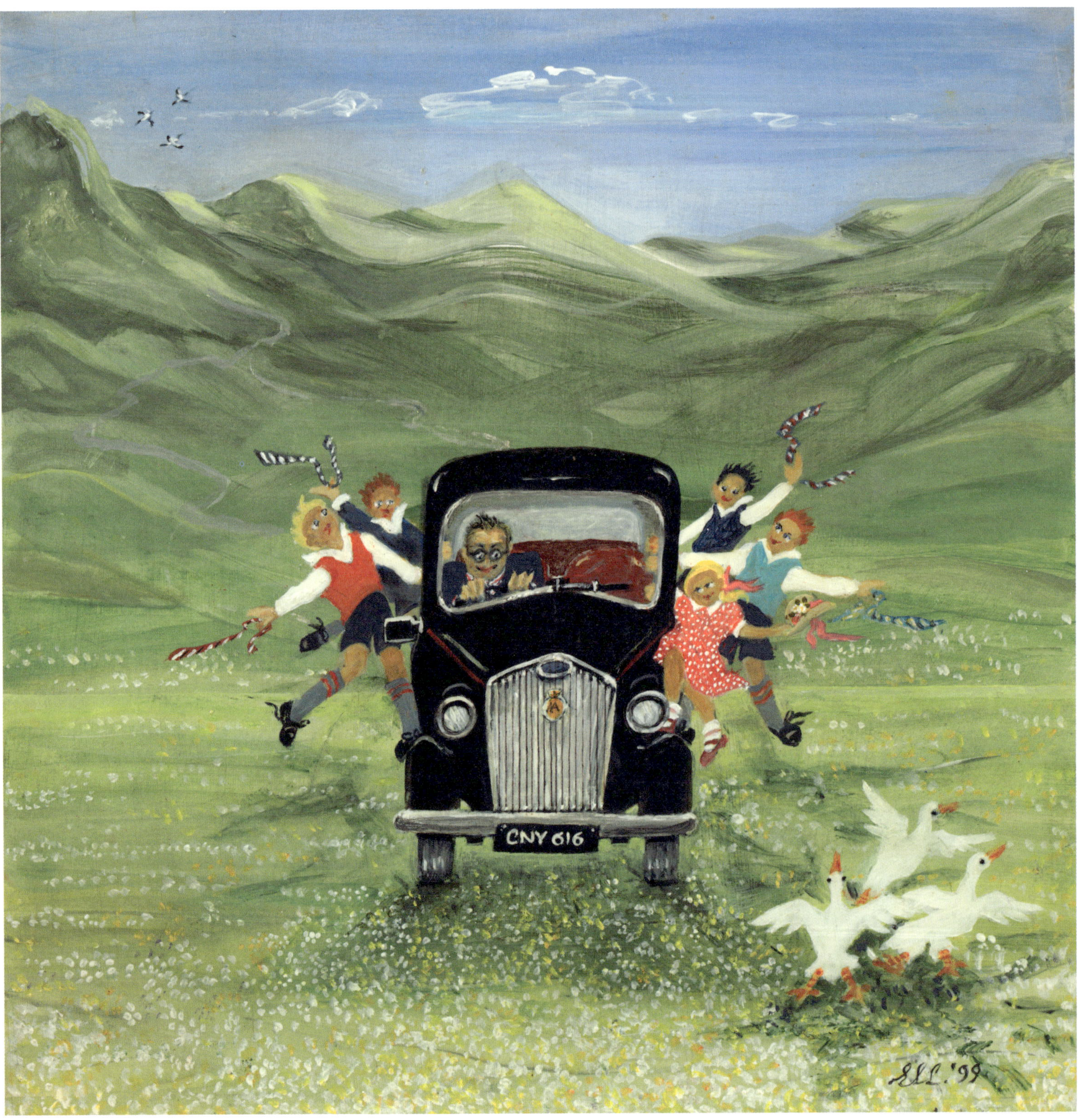

GANGSTERS

In this scene we can see the contrast in the children's lives compared to Mamgu's life, her own childhood. I don't suppose she ever had as much fun as we had, although childhood often carries its own inner protection from too much comprehension of the enormity of adult responsibilities and struggles. So here we are, her son, my father, is driving our Ford 8, CNY 616, round and round in a meadow whilst we children stand on the running boards, balancing on one leg and clinging on by our fingernails. My father used to do the same up in the farmyard, its submerged boulders challenging our wits as we were hurled from side to side, up and down.

The scenario is 'gangsters', inspired by the black and white films we saw at children's matinees down in the town. These were a rare, ecstatic treat, made so by stopping at a sweetshop and buying a six-squared bar of delicious milk chocolate, each pair of squares filled with cream of different flavours – strawberry was the favourite. The Ford 8 merry-go-round was quite dangerous but it was lovely to frighten yourself by fearing you were going to fall off. My father seemed to get in the spirit of it, being a child at heart and a rather reckless one at that, but it meant that for a brief moment we were all converted from a crowd of Welsh farm children to a sinister gang of Chicago gangsters, the silver screen having a great influence on all our lives.

CONKER FIGHTS

Everybody knows about conkers, or maybe not everyone knows about conkers anymore. Here we have the bushy horse chestnut tree with its surprising inedible fruit – the nut is contained within a round and spiny green shell. We prise that off, or it falls off on the ground when ripe. Out pops the most beautiful shiny, slippery-surfaced nut, 'conker-coloured' – a brilliantly rich brown – which we take home to dry. Some children soaked them in vinegar to make them harder, claiming to have secret recipes which would make them champions in conker fights. Then we would get a metal skewer and bore a little hole right through the centre to the other side, then thread a long piece of string through that, tying a good knot to secure it. Thus armed, we chose an opponent and fought knuckle-bruising battles by aiming one conker at another until the weaker one shattered, its owner the loser. I must say I struggled playing conkers with my boy cousins because they were so good at it, aiming determinedly with no mercy.

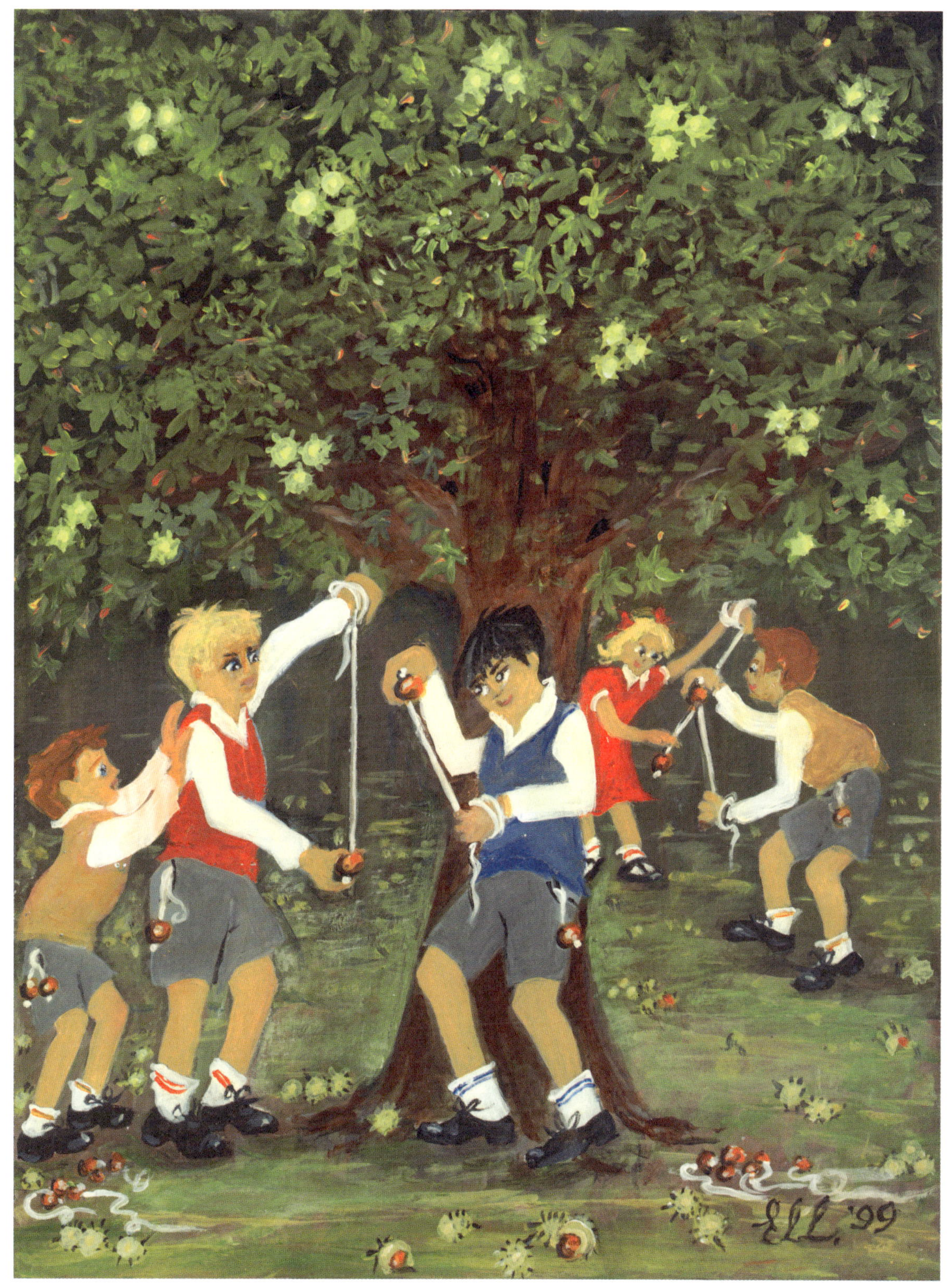

CHURNING THE BUTTER

Here we see the process and philosophy of how best to produce a few pounds of butter with the least individual personal effort. The oddness of seeing a wooden butter churn standing out in the open air at a spot which had lots of toing and froing of people had method in its madness, based upon the family mantra, 'never be seen doing nothing, if it's only picking up sticks for the fire, transposed in this case to 'never cross the graig yard without stopping to give the butter churn a turn or two' – many hands make light work. My grandmother Mamgu was in charge, naturally, only she measuring the ingredients of thick yellow cream from the top of the milk and a modicum of salt, the aim being to pound and churn them until solidified and turned to butter. This took many hours by hand, hence the location of the churn and the obligation of all and sundry to stop and give the handle as many turns as possible before continuing on their way. The more solid the mix became, the harder the effort to turn the handle. Competition between the boys being ever-present, as usual my brother was best, he having sent away for the Charles Atlas bodybuilding course advertised in one of his comics, C.A., claiming he'd 'once been a seven-stone weakling'.

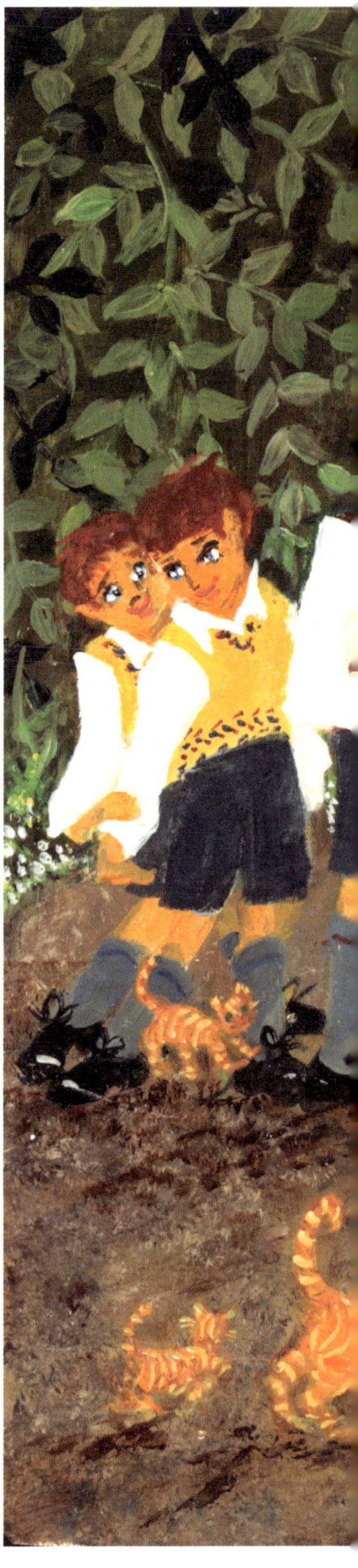

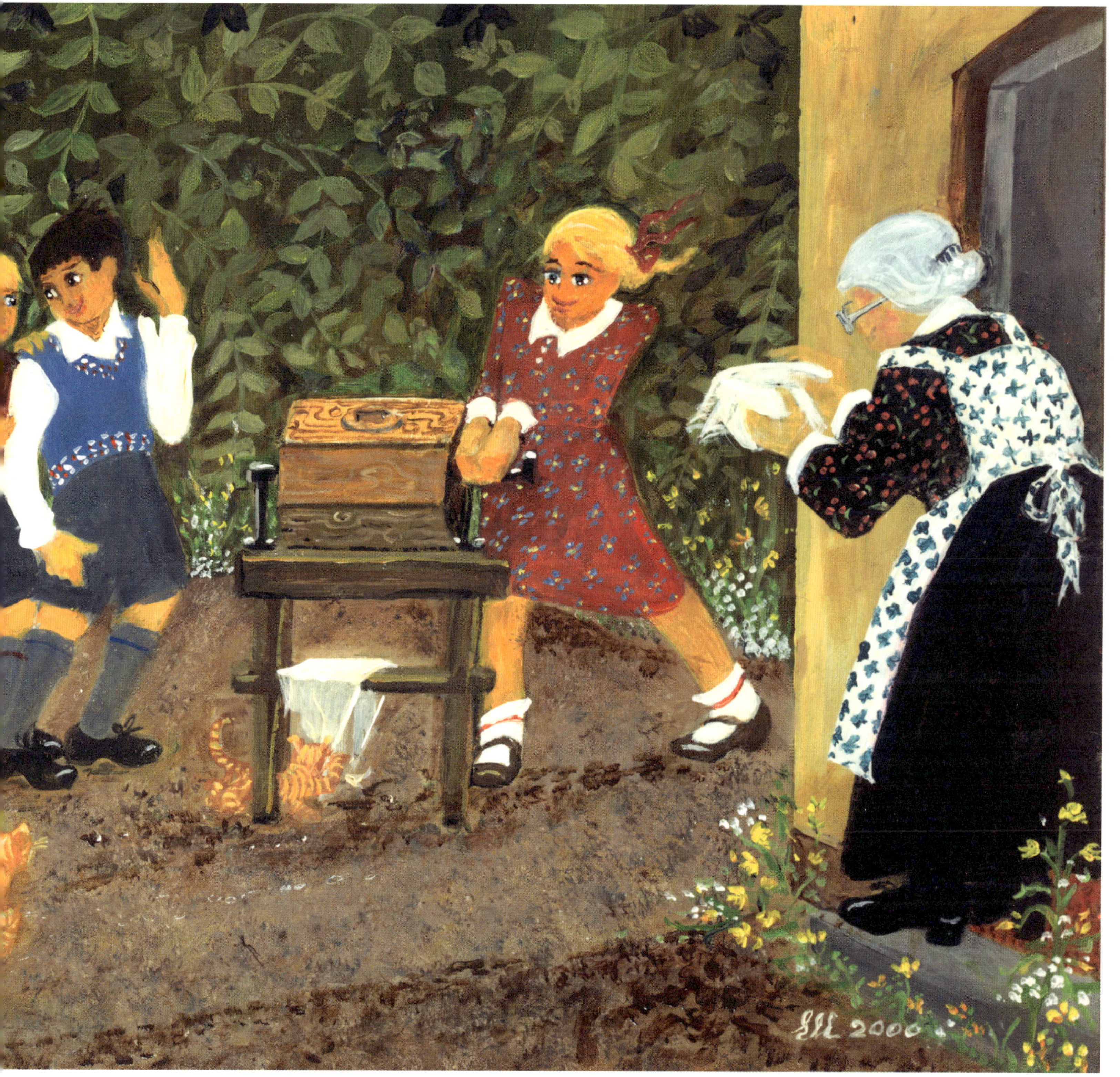
JH 2000

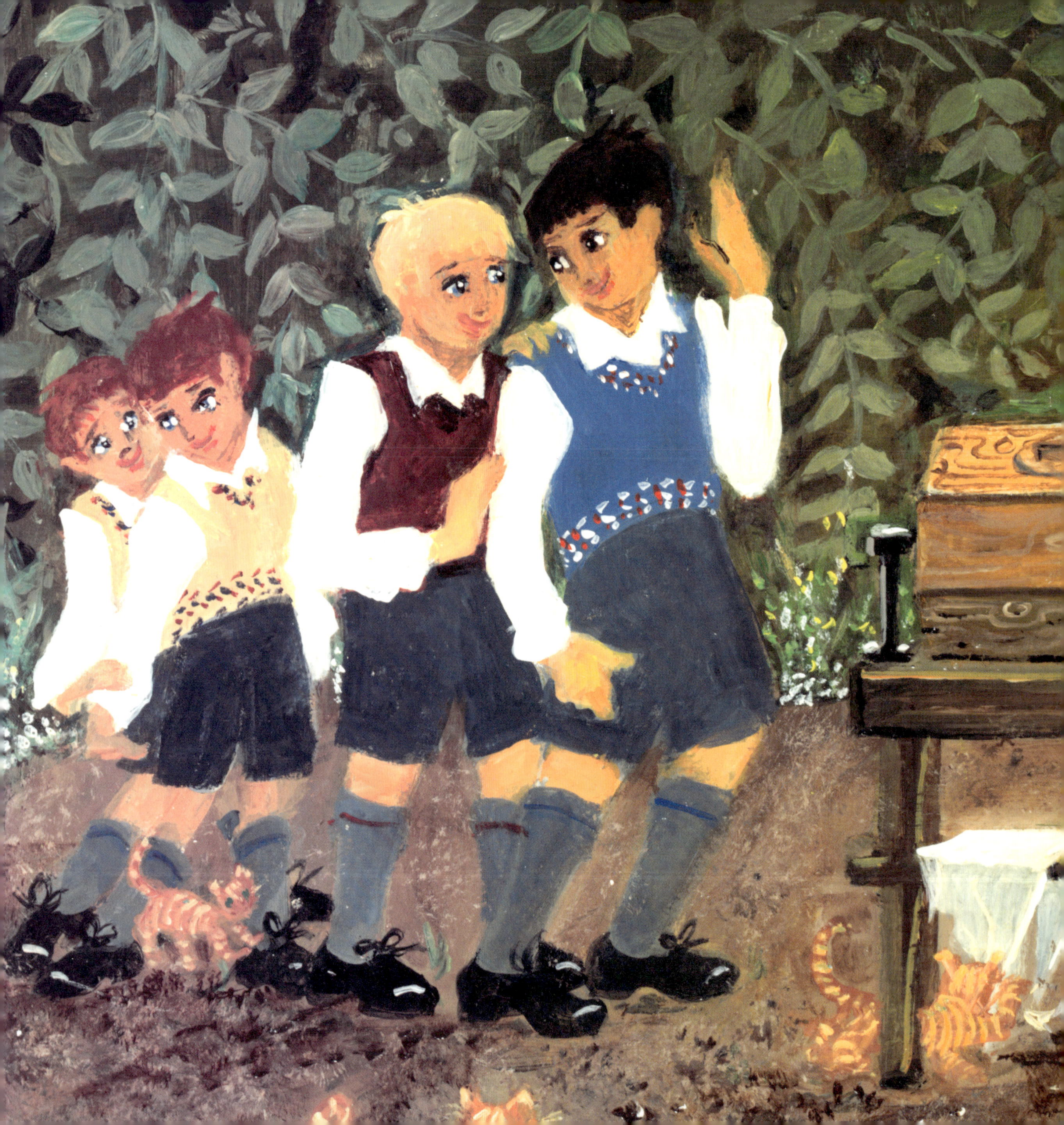

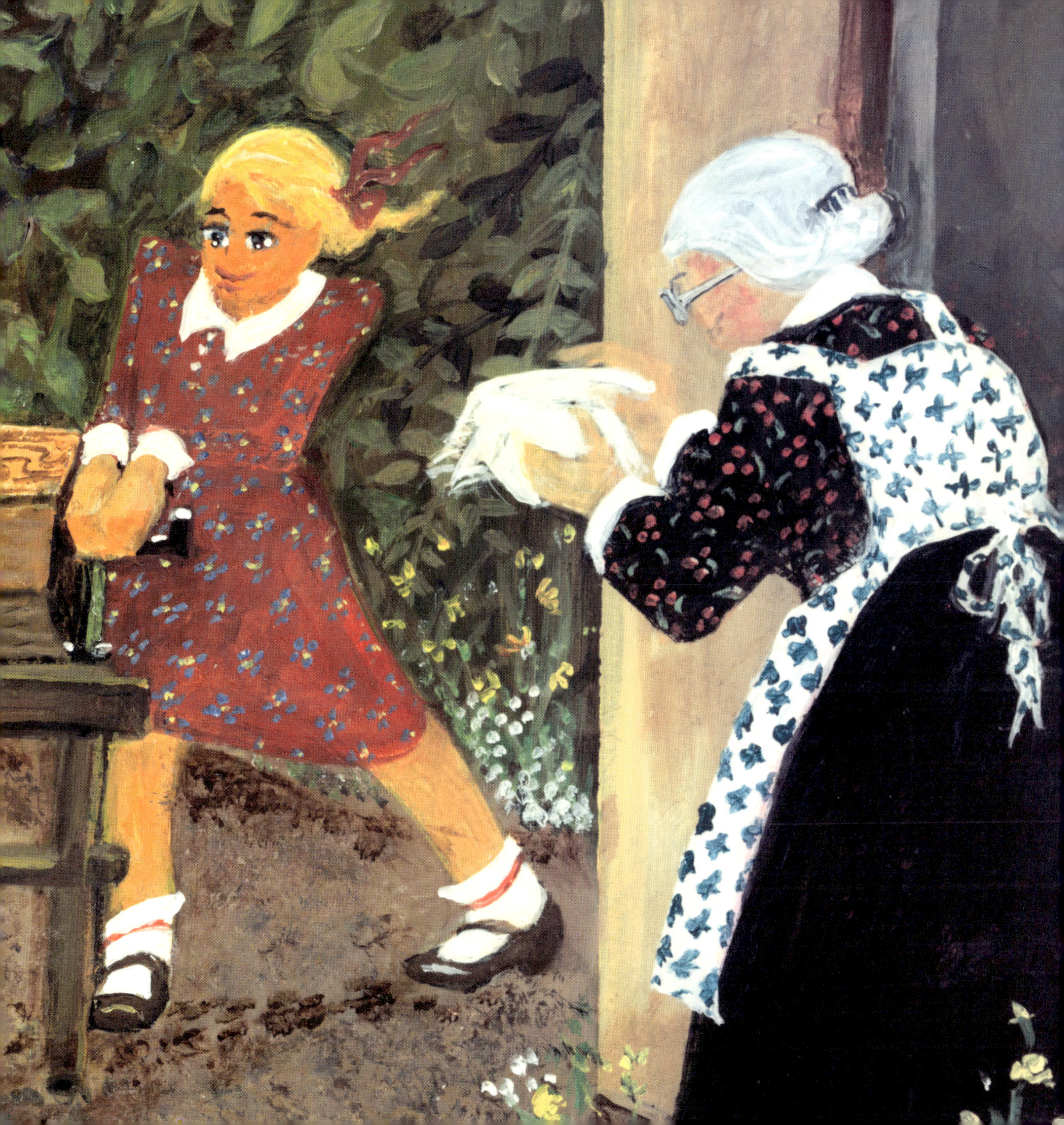

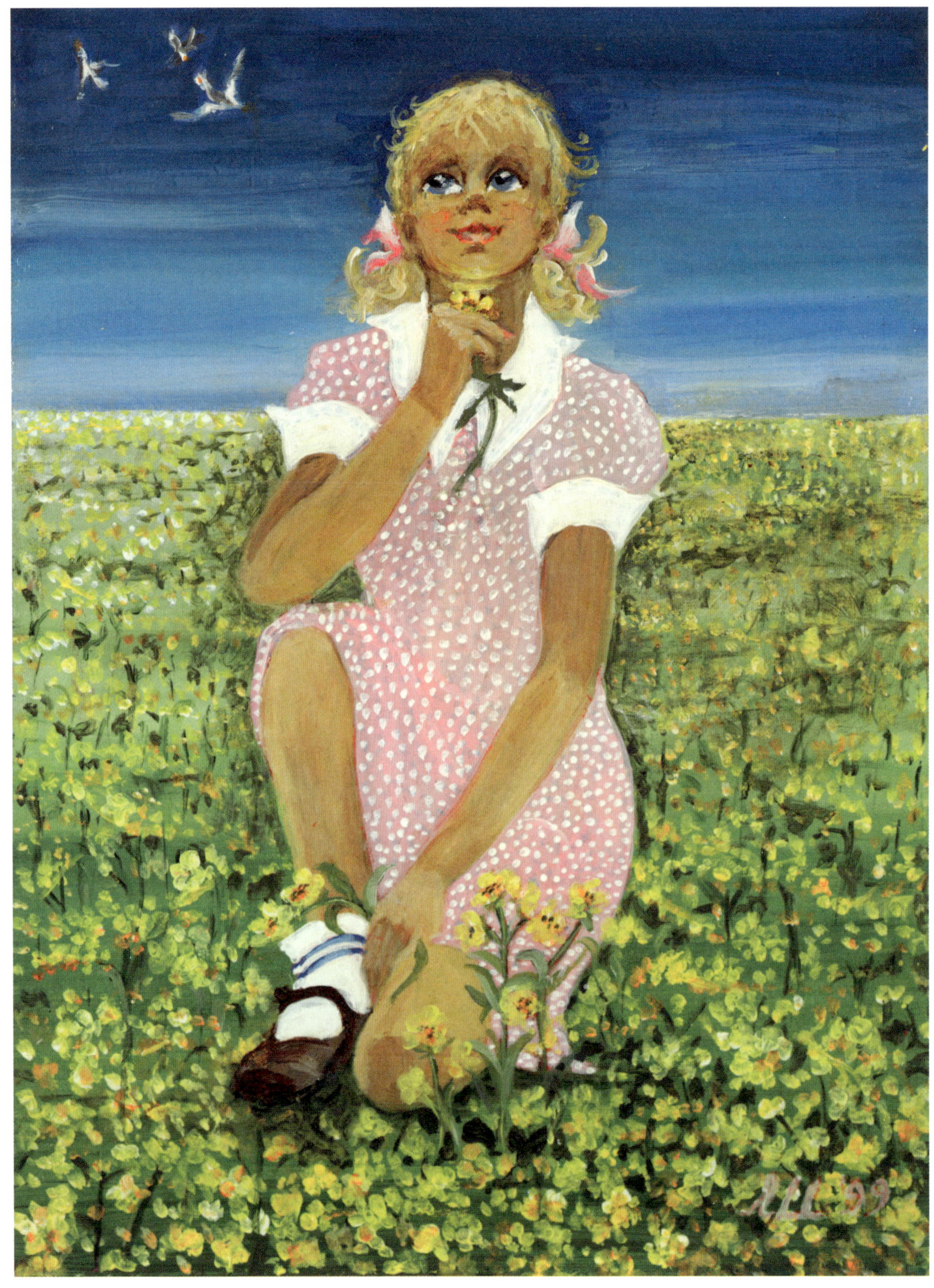

DO YOU LIKE BUTTER?

The subject here is the buttercup, which flourished in the fields everywhere on the farm where I grew up. I was fortunate in having great freedom to roam about in safety and thus spent many happy hours peering at insects of all kinds, let alone wildflowers. The buttercup, of course, is the barometer by which we judge whether a person likes butter or not. It is simply plucked and the vibrant yellow flower held under the chin, varying degrees of luminous reflection being cast onto the skin – a little game we could not resist playing, should the presence of a buttercup and an idle moment coincide.

FOXGLOVES

This painting concerns the foxglove, one of the tallest and most impressive of wildflowers. Folklore passed down through the generations has somehow invented the bizarre image of foxes wearing these blossoms as gloves for their paws. Bearing in mind that the foxglove is the source of digitalis, a drug used to stimulate the heart, then for all we know foxes discovered that by dipping their paws into a blossom they would pick up some digitalis and be able to run faster in pursuit of their prey or to escape some predator. Imagination is a wonderful thing and children have lots of it. My own imagination had me cast as a lady at a dance, prancing around with elegant gestures – the belle of the ball.

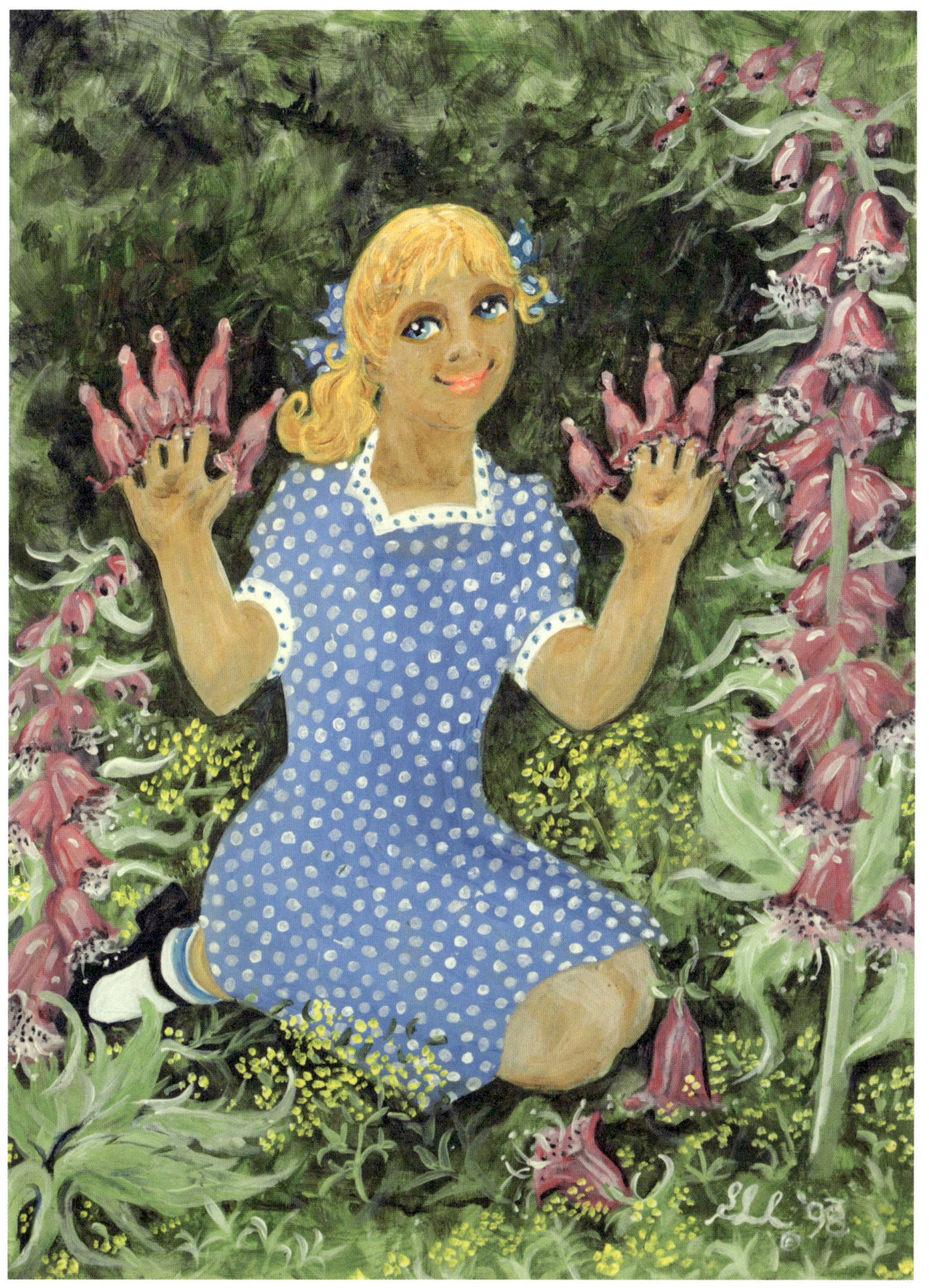

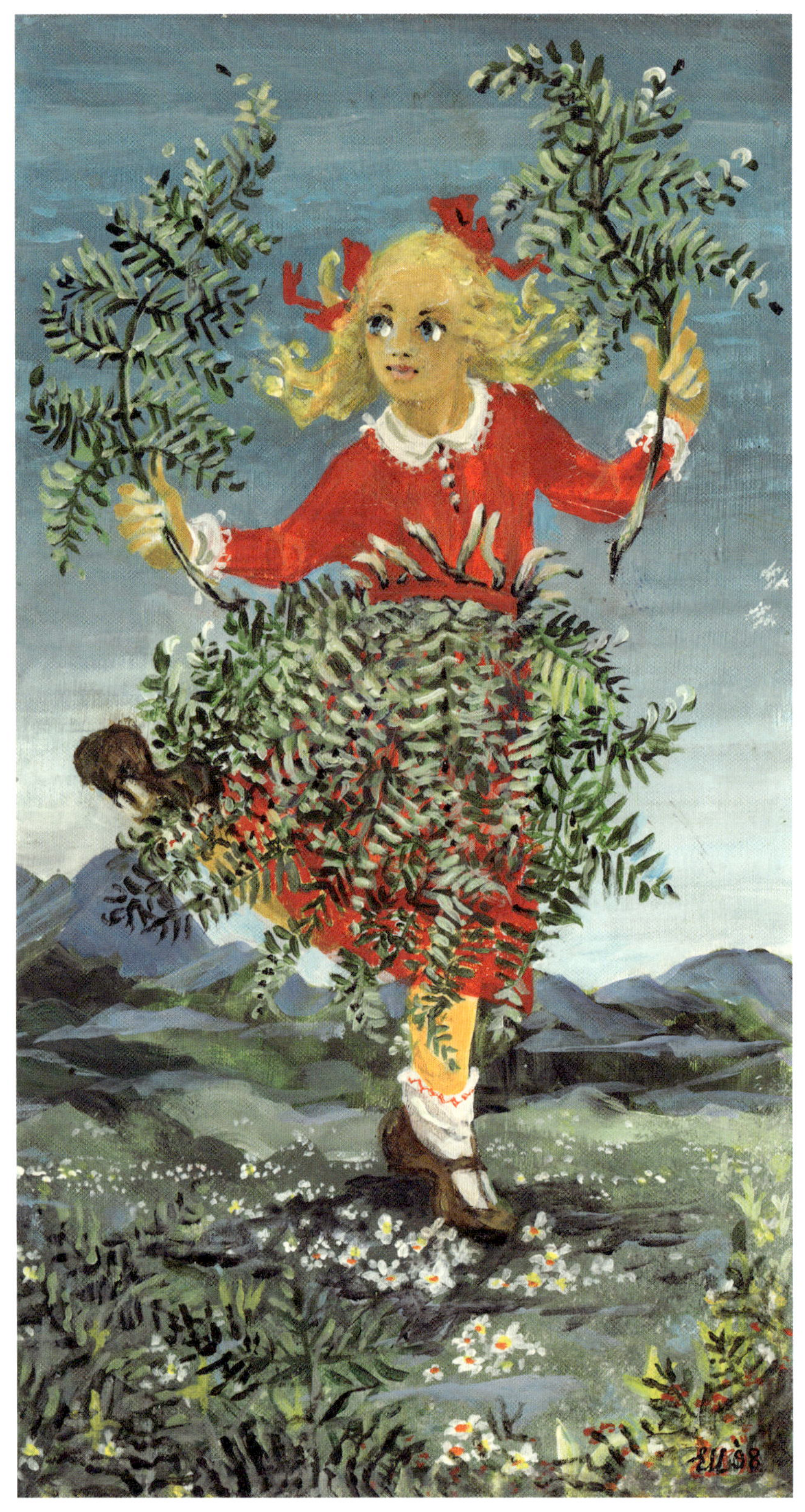

FERN DANCE

The walk home from school, always alone and on foot, rain or shine, offered countless opportunities for my imagination. The route included, on the last lap, two big fields to cross and a good mile uphill of narrow, boulder-strewn lane overhung with hedgerows bursting with wildlife, in particular birds' nests and birdsong. It was a happy experience guaranteed to wipe out any unhappy experience in the classroom, like a smack on the leg for chattering and giggling – a weakness of mine. Ferns were my great delight, rising in musky-scented profusion all around, their colours changing swiftly and dramatically with each season, a rich palette of greens and golds and russet brown.

It was the roots I loved, pulling them up from deep in the earth, their succulent, spear-like white and black stalks just perfect for bending and looping around my belt so that the ferns could hang like a crinoline dress to dance the rest of the way home with. I was always late getting home, but nobody worried, except one farmer had to be asked to keep his geese and ganders in at teatime, they having attacked me once too often, leaving painful red pinches on my back from their beaks. They were renowned for being better than any guard dog.

GOOD NEWS

This is all about Mr Middleton – we adored and
worshipped and idolised Mr Middleton. He had two
jobs: the morning one was as our postman, and he'd
come all the way up to the farm in all weathers, even
blizzards, when everyone else had gone home early
from work or school. He carried a prize to me once
– a suitcase full of Christmas fare won in a raffle –
puddings, mincemeat, a cake, crystallised fruits, all
sunk deep in shredded, shiny red paper. The suitcase,
though made of cardboard, lasted years and went
on many a holiday with us. Mr Middleton was never
without the widest, kindest, happiest smile I have ever
seen, dear Mr Middleton.

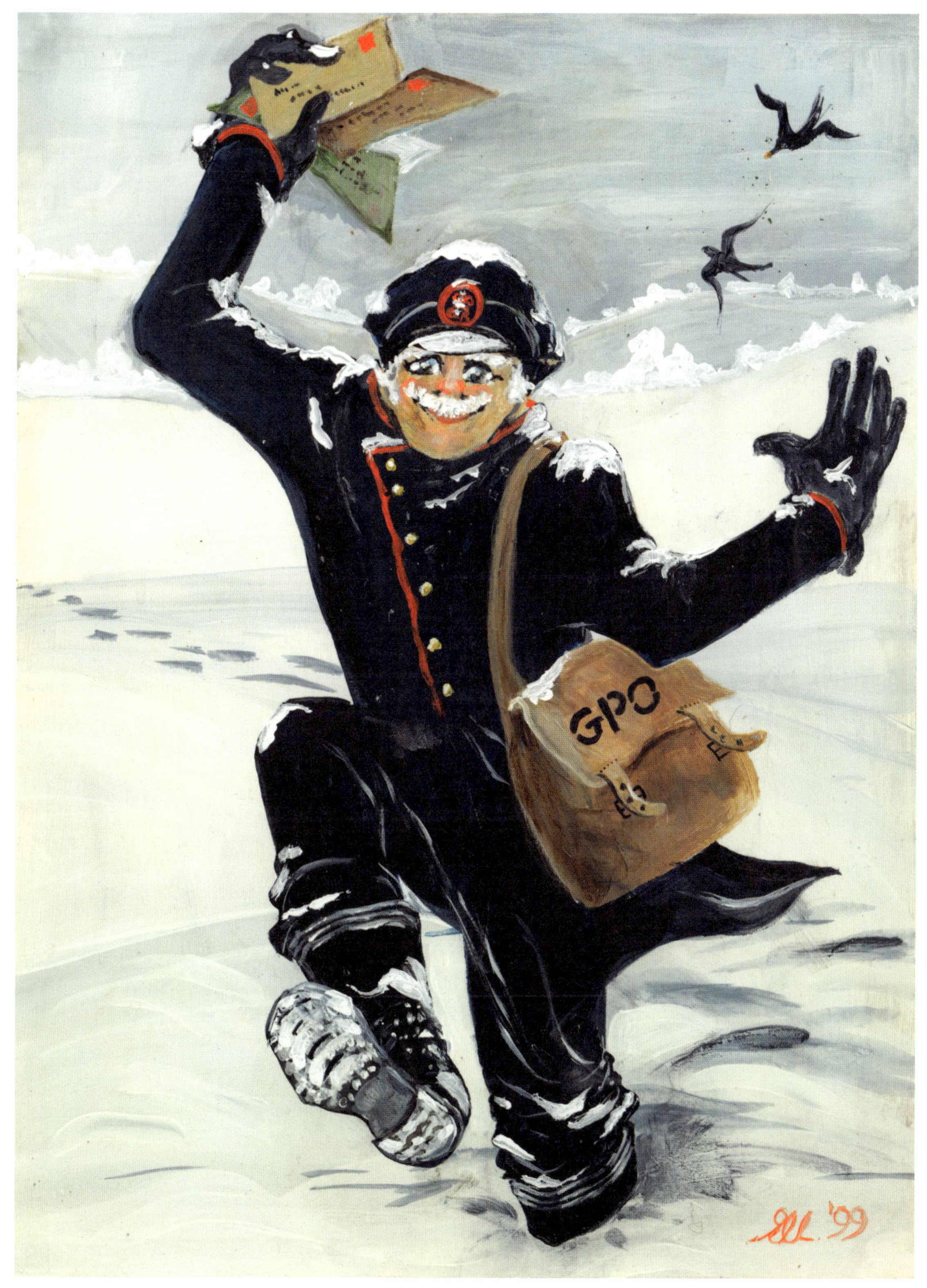GPO

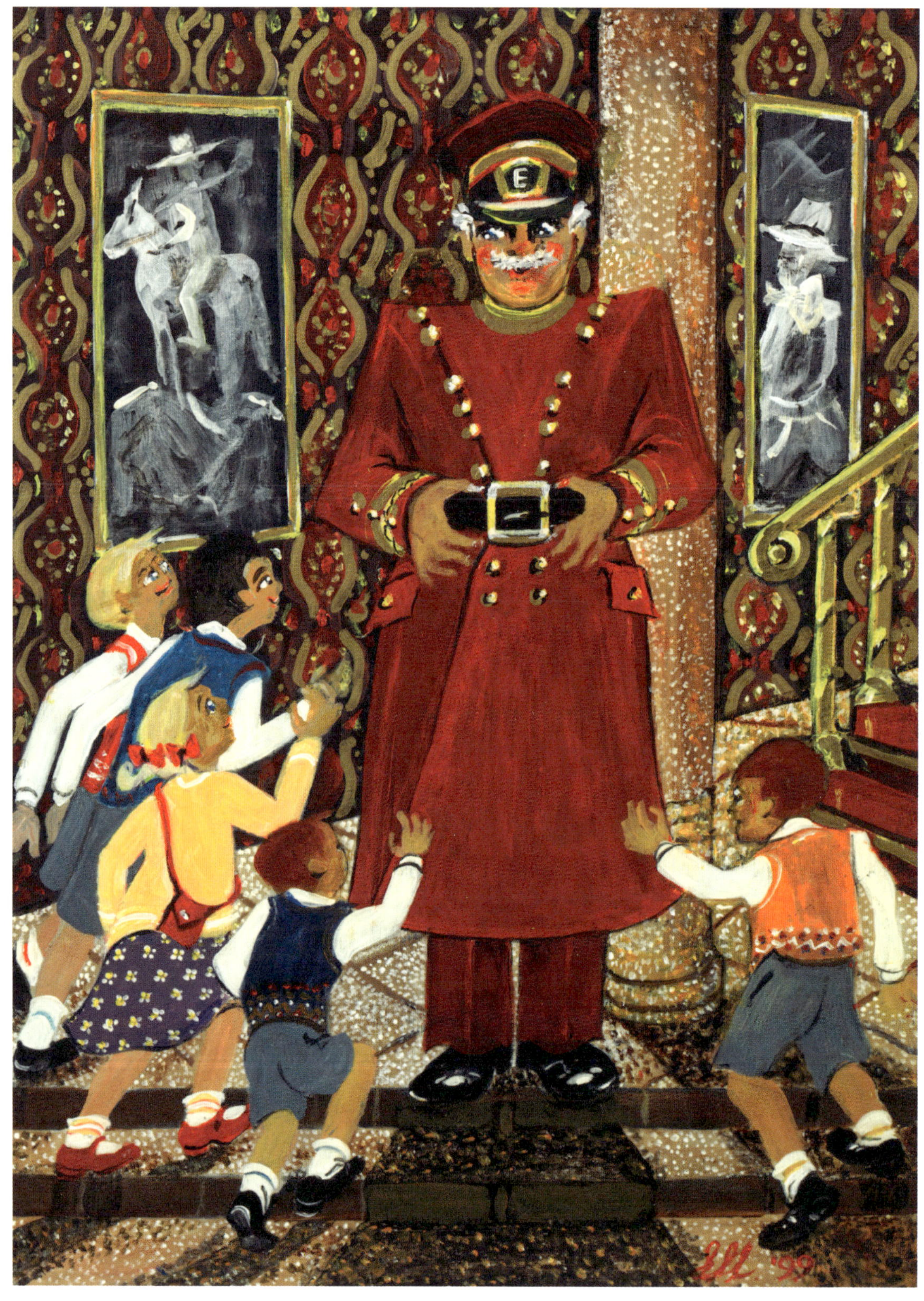

COMMISSIONAIRE

This is Mr Middleton in his other role, dressed up in his
scarlet and gold commissionaire's uniform, controlling
the crowds rushing through the plush foyer of the
local cinema where we cousins were introduced to
the black and white films of gangsters, cowboys and
Shirley Temple with her blond curls and singing voice.
The excitement of being plunged into darkness as the
cinema organ rose from under the stage, its organist
playing popular tunes in crescendo, coloured lights
transforming the scene magically, we children greedily
tearing open our bars of chocolate bought at the
sweetshop outside, was such a thrill that we wouldn't
have called the King our uncle. And there was dear Mr
Middleton, presiding over it all.

LUCKY ESCAPE

This involves an escapade of my brother's on the farm. Captain, Farmer and the other carthorses had their own stables on the perimeter of the yard, in which they ate and slept in warm comfort, their supply of golden hay stored in the stable loft and distributed to their manger by forking it through holes in the floorboards of the loft. The boys, having tired of tunnelling through the vast haystack up in the barnyard, risking their lives if a tunnel collapsed, went looking for further fun. The stable loft provided it, the game being to run its length and jump over every hole as it came up. My brother misjudged and fell straight through over a storage area for sharp tools and other paraphernalia. Luckily, his jumper caught on a big rusty hook, suspending him there, unable to move. The hook could have injured him badly.

The alarm was raised by his cousins and the uncles raced to the stable and lifted my brother safely down. He received a good shaking by the shoulders and a telling off, all in Welsh. Lucky escapes were the norm for life on the farm, such as when a small cousin wandered into the field where Prince the bull was grazing. Usually he was locked up and I always raced past his shed at top speed, since he was rampaging about inside it, the old wooden doors shaking with angry thuds. The sight of a very small boy toddling about happily in a field where a snorting bull eyed him balefully is enough to freeze anyone to the spot, but someone raised yet another alarm, and uncles raced (they were very fit) to the rescue, snatching the child from the very jaws of death. The child himself yelled at the top of his voice at being robbed of his fun.

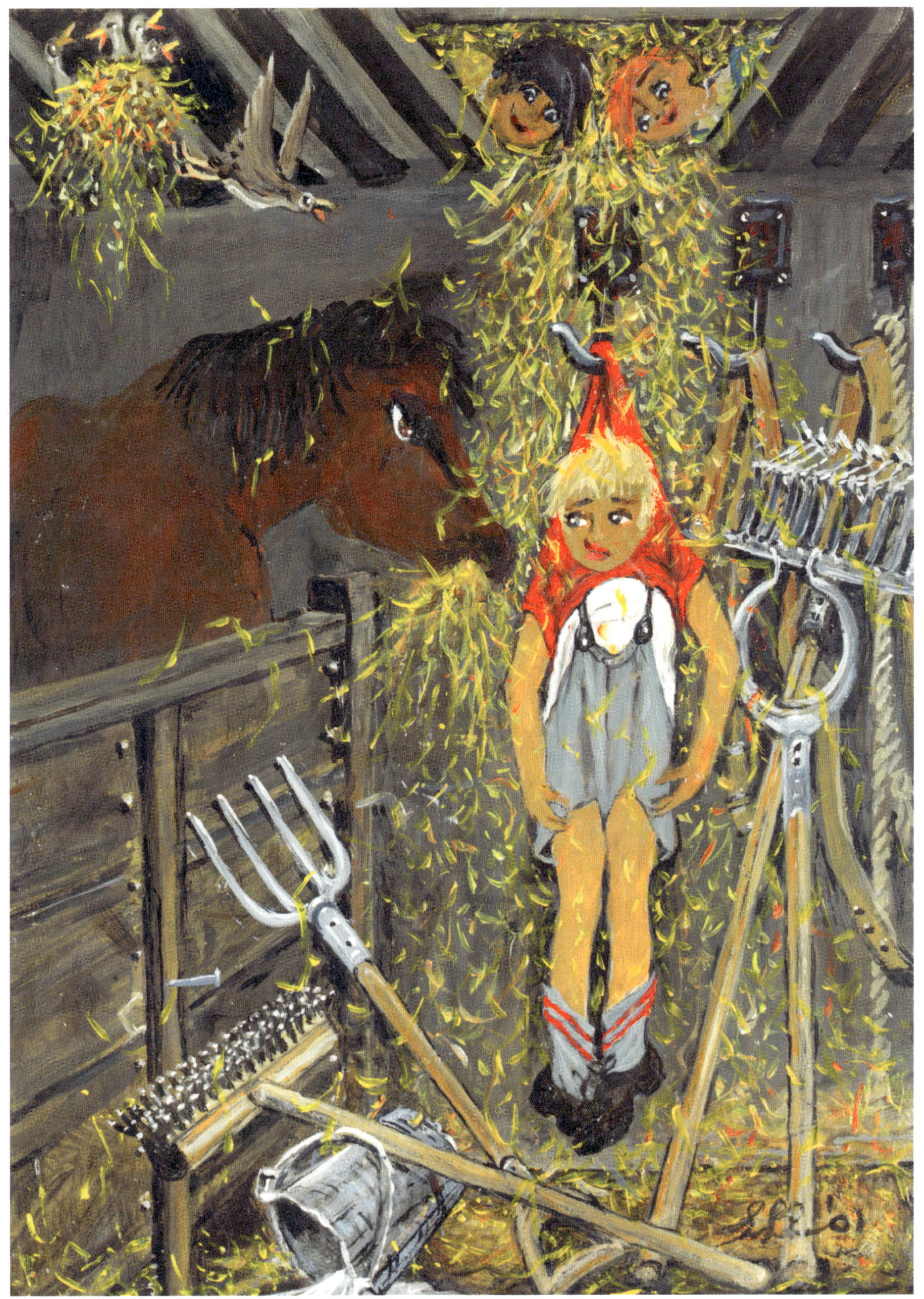

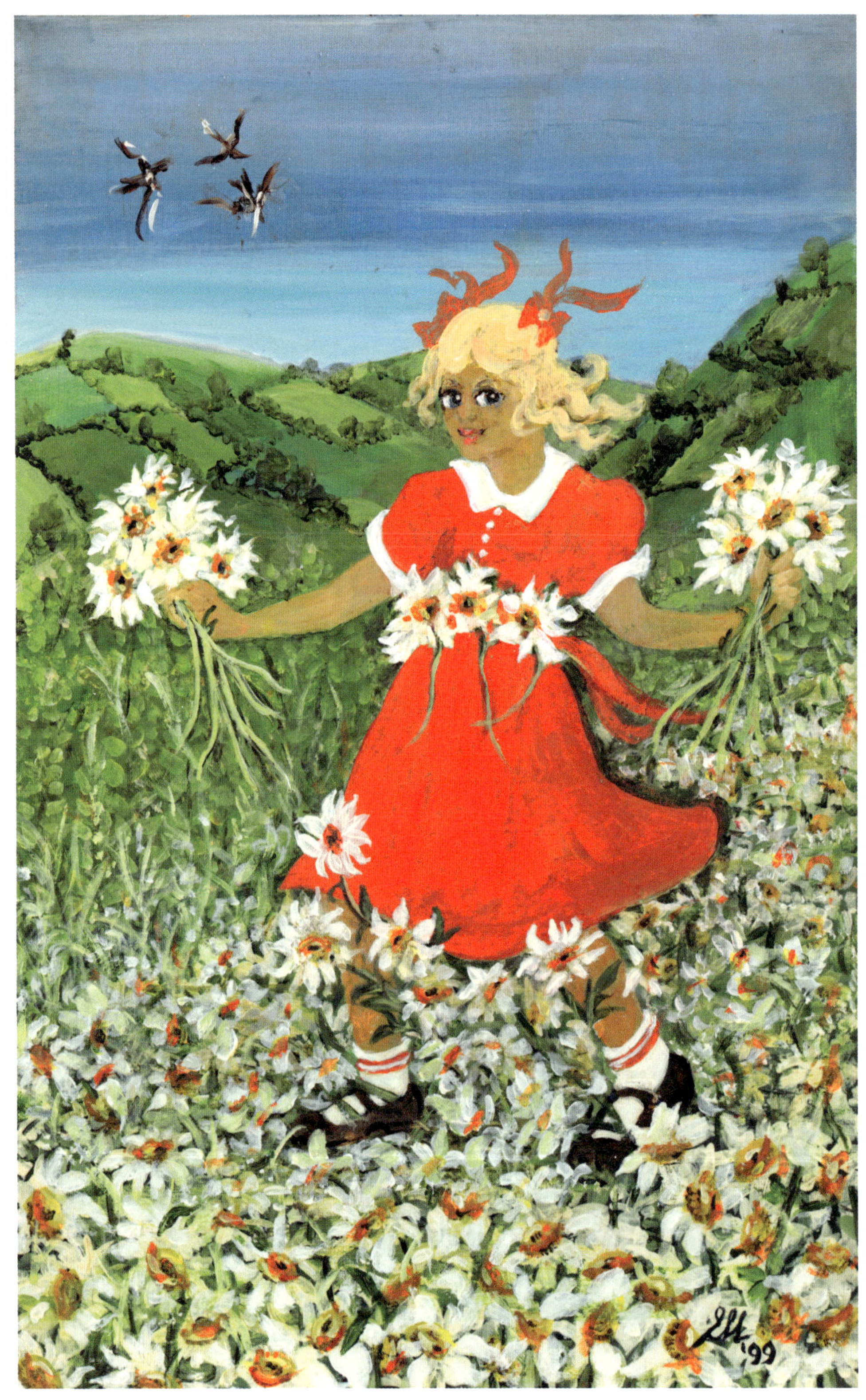

DAISIES

Dog daisies, those tall, simple, graceful, lighthearted flowers of the field, abounded everywhere, so that in summertime I was almost permanently adorned with garlands of one kind or another, pretending I was a dancer on a beautiful stage somewhere, like the church hall down in the town, where I, with others, had dressed up as gypsies to sing and dance: 'Gypsies we, light and free, through the world we roam...' Mostly I ran through seas of dog daisies taller than myself, dizzy with nature's pure magic.

MAKE BELIEVE

I was the only girl living on the farm amongst five cousins, which meant that most of the time I had to rely on myself for entertainment of the feminine variety. Dressing up came high on the list, but it had to be exciting, like pretending to be a Native American. My mother's cyclamen-coloured lipstick, frowned upon by the matriarchal Mamgu, my grandmother, was exactly right for painting on like terrifying warpaint, whilst the headgear came from a stall in the market, additional beads being added from my mother's collection. The feathers were actually made out of paper, I think. Wild scenery and tall grasses became magnified tenfold and occasionally the boys joined in, making bowers and ambushing each other with bloodcurdling yells, but I, the self-appointed Chief, remained dignified and aloof in true tribal style.

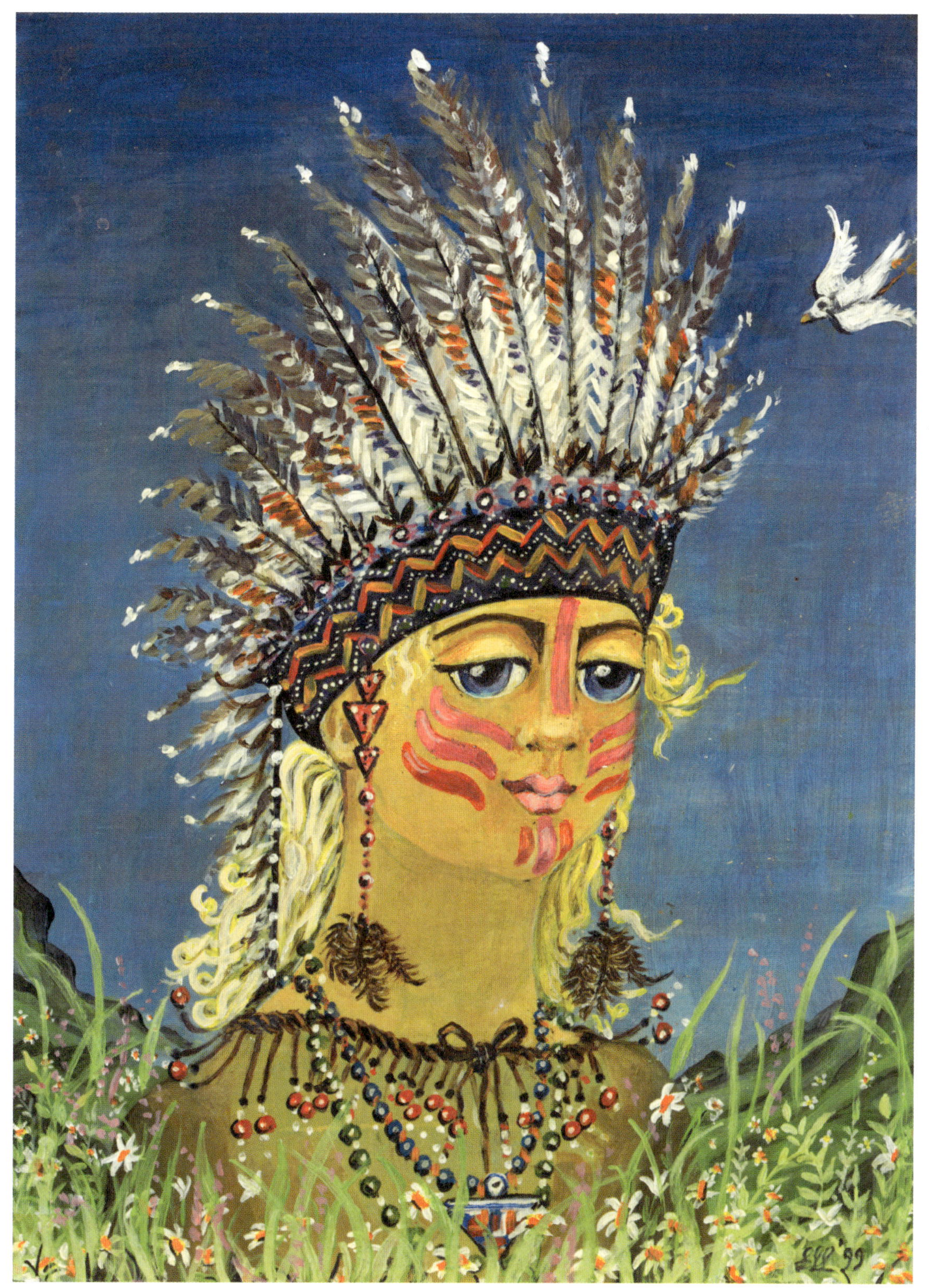

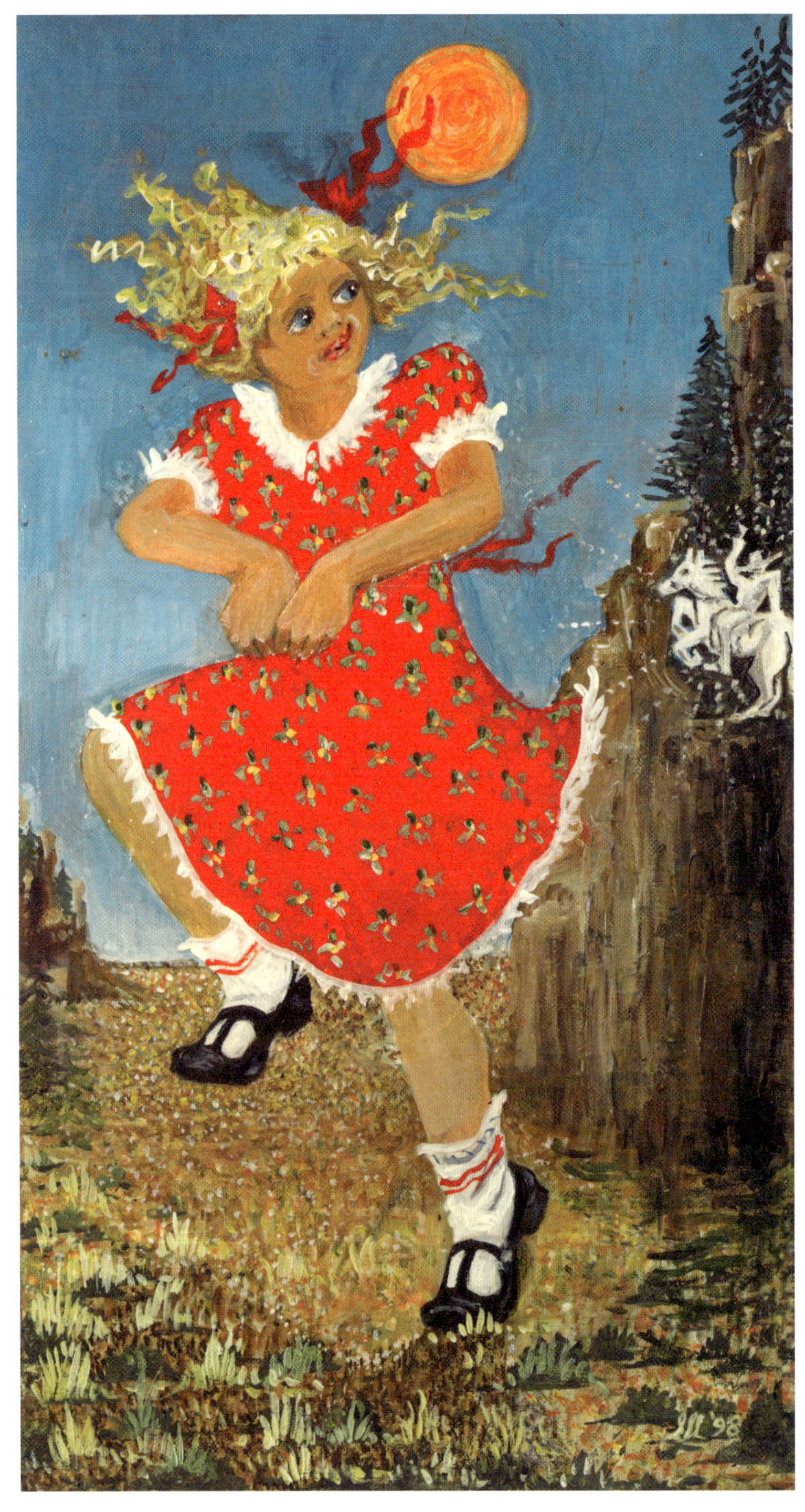

ROY ROGERS

The advent of heroes on the silver screen of Saturday matinees inspired longing on my part to be Roy Rogers, with his horse, Trigger. I fell deeply in love with Roy Rogers – his twinkling eyes and dimpled cheeks, his wide, white-toothed smile and the acrobatic tricks he could do with Trigger, the most beautiful horse I had ever seen, nothing like our dear old farm horses, Farmer and Captain, love them though I did, as carthorses. Off I would gallop on my imaginary Trigger across imaginary prairies, dressed in my mind's eye in the female equivalent of Roy Rogers' white outfit – a diaphanous, star-spangled frock, right down to my feet, silver all over, dainty white boots and stars encircling my head – I was totally carried away in a fantasy which felt so real that I could hardly let go of it without pain. He would sing too, and play guitar – the hero of my childhood dreams.

ARRIVAL

Whenever we travelled to stay with Mamam at her tiny terraced house near the wild west coast, it was another aunt of mine who always met us. Of the one thing we could be sure – we would receive a welcome like no other, for she had the happy energy of a bird in full flight, joyful. Even her appearance made me think of a bird (or was it the way she moved?), but apart from that her human attributes were those of a loving nature and a generous, compassionate spirit. Her husband was my barber uncle, he of the secret silver sixpence pressed ungrudgingly into we children's hands. They had twins, a boy and a girl, as well as an older son who was sweet and gentle as an angel. The twin girl was my favourite of all my cousins, daring and mischievous and always laughing happily. She was fearless on a swing, terrifyingly so, and likewise when we paddled for hours in the pure, sparkling river running down to the sea, its bed lined with flat, pale pebbles which we skimmed from one bank to the other, the pebble bouncing across the surface of the water or sinking like the stone it was.

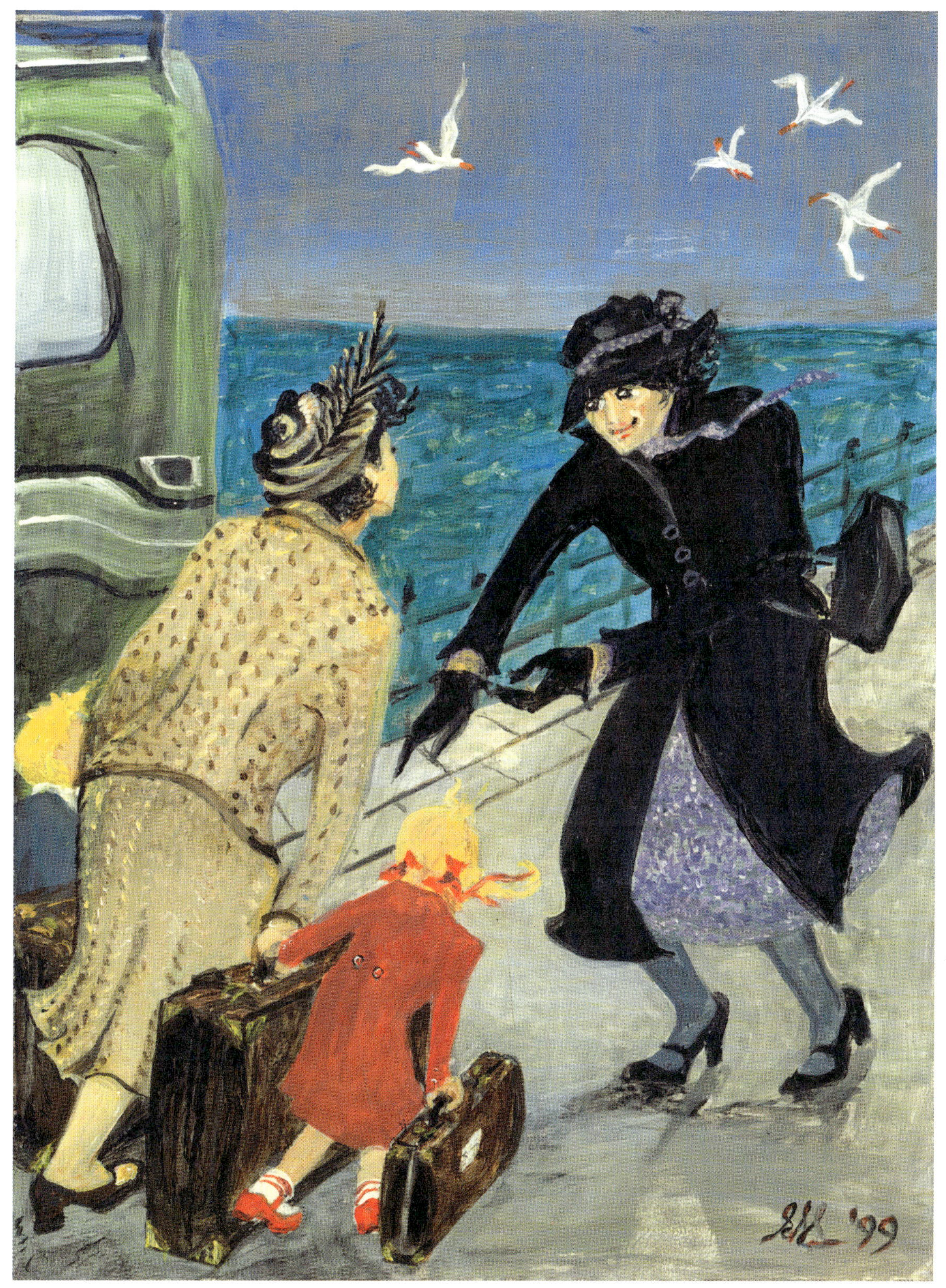

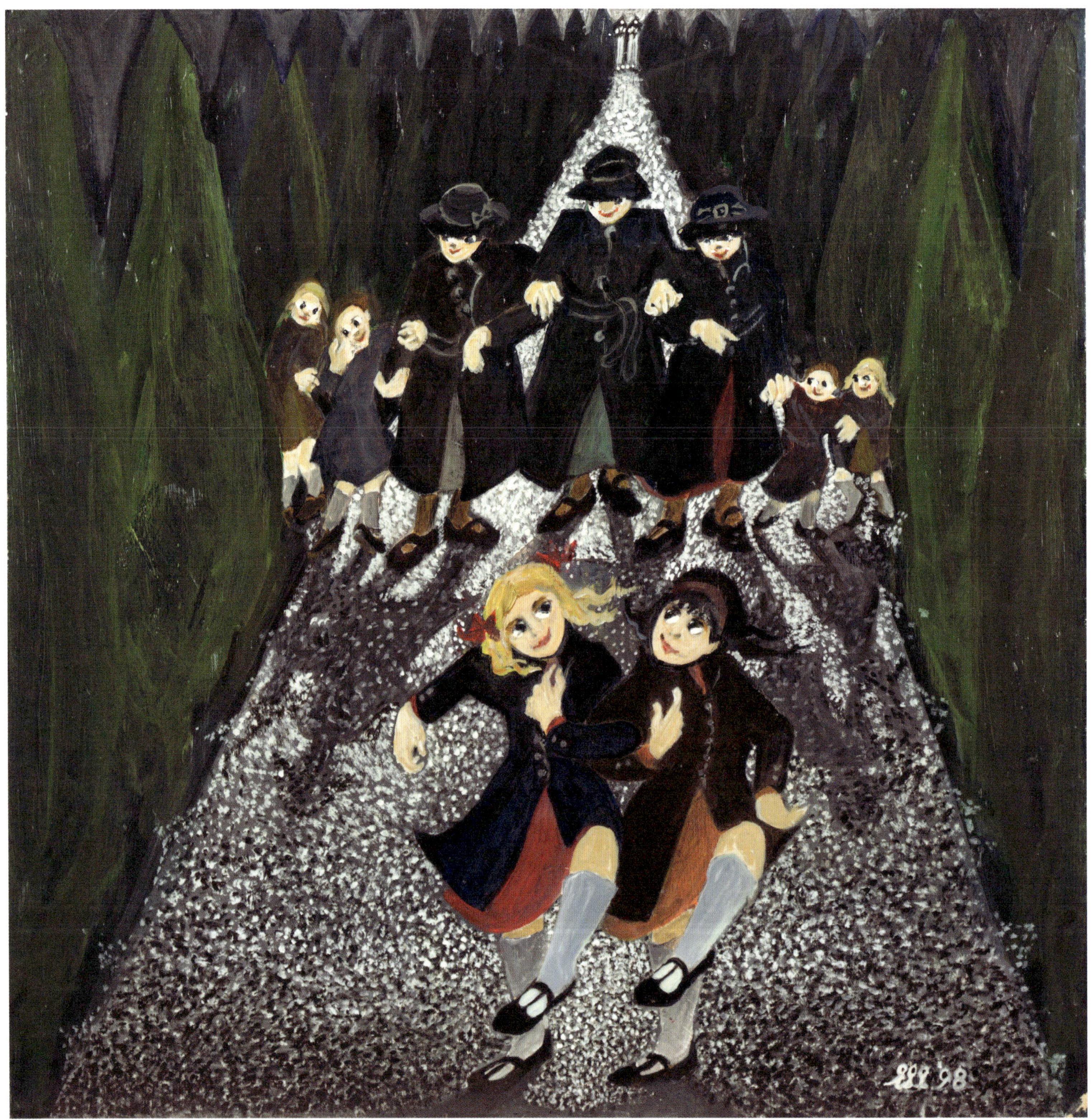

WALKING HOME

This depicts the challenge of taking a short cut home through the cemetery after dark, following a visit to the cinema, aunts, cousins, assorted. It was my spinster aunt who was the main source of all the fun, her single status seeming to have kept her young at heart, even though she was living on some kind of war pension from the First World War, compensation for having all her fingertips cut off by a guillotine whilst working in a munitions factory.

The deaths of millions of young men in that war meant millions of young women had no one to marry and build families with. Her generosity was humbling, bearing in mind her low income, although she lived with Mamam and Papa. Treats for us children could not have brought more joy than a visit to Disneyland for today's children – it was the spirit of the thing.

She also excelled at knitting, winning competitions nationwide, fingertips or no fingertips. Parcels came flying through our door with gifts from her for me, jumpers, cardigans, socks, hats, gloves, boleros. Many were copies of those worn by the young princesses Elizabeth and Margaret.

Sometimes I would stare sadly at her poor maimed little fingers, the skin drawn so tight and red and thin over the bones of her middle joints. She was so brave and never expressed pity for herself. She just generated fun, like scratching at our bedroom door pretending to be a ghost, but we all knew it was her because you could tell it was a fork she was scratching with, she having no fingernails. This was usually the finale after the short cut home through the cemetery when we children had gone to bed.

BARBER SHOP

The first thing my bird-like aunt would do after greeting us at the bus or railway station was to show us children to her husband, my uncle. He was a barber, and we entered the tiny, dark salon with trepidation always, because the next thing we would get was a lavish squirt of powerfully scented brilliantine from a mystical looking glass bottle covered with silk netting in a bright colour. From there we would be proudly introduced to the customers and welcomed warmly. Teasing came next, like asking me, 'Whose little boy are you, then?' Finally we would exit, but not before a tiny, warm silver sixpence was pressed secretly into each child's hand – half my beloved uncle's profit for the day, no doubt.

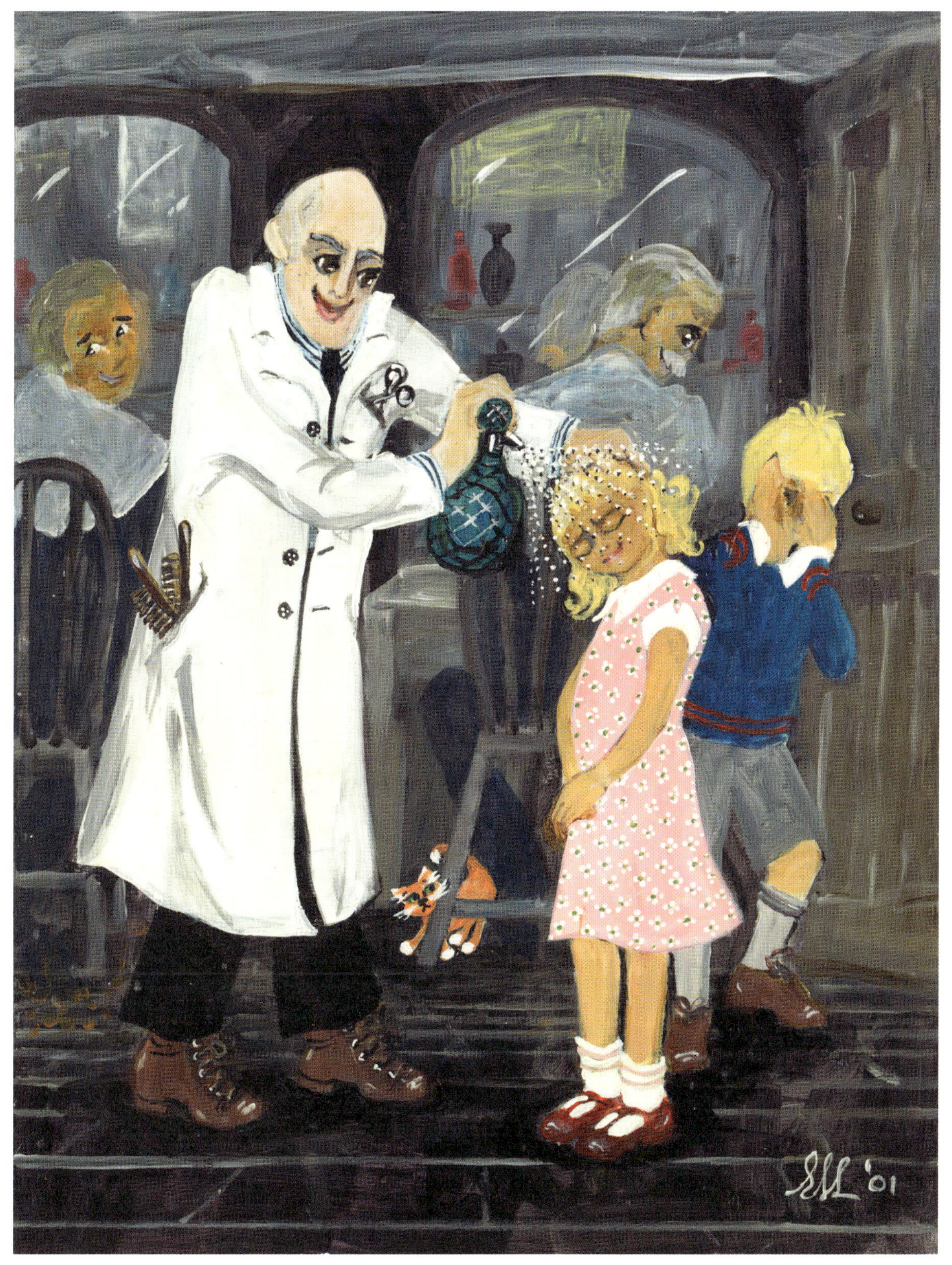

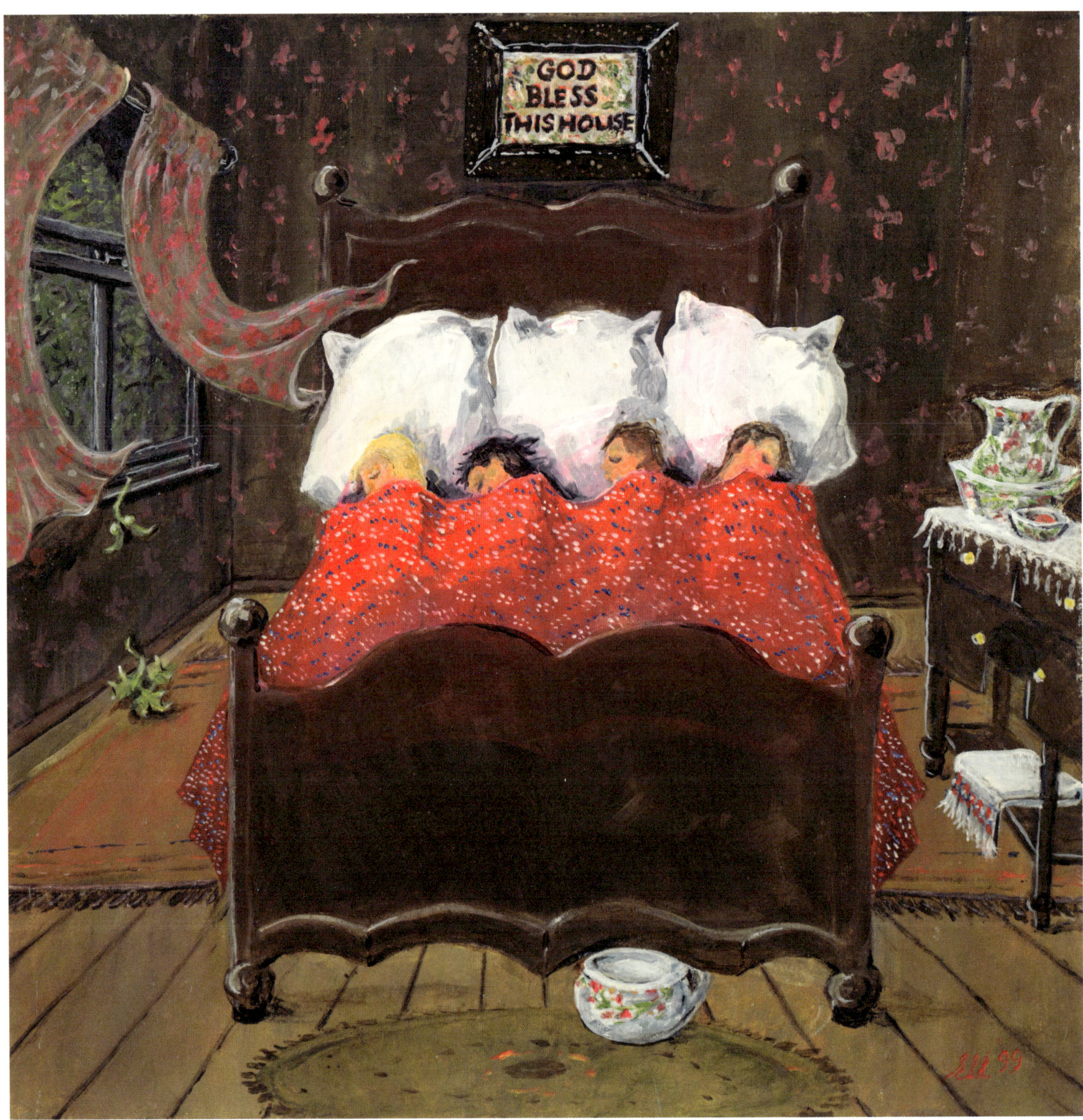

GOD
BLESS
THIS HOUSE

GOD BLESS THIS HOUSE

Here we cousins are, some of us, asleep like birds in a nest in Papa and Mamam's huge double bed. A wooden bar down the middle under the mattress was stuffed full with eiderdown direct from the eider duck, whose home was the Arctic and who knew a thing or two as to how to keep warm. The huge, fat pillows generated warmth around our heads too, a necessity due to the window always being left open a little, no matter how strong the gale blowing in from the sea. Huge sycamore trees grew outside, their propellor seeds landing on the cold linoleum with a 'splat', just like wet fish being landed at the harbour. Lighting was by candle, held safe in a sparkling brass candleholder strictly under control of our aunt. No bathroom meant the presence of a flowered china chamberpot hidden discreetly under the bed. A wool embroidered tapestry hung over the bed requesting God to 'Bless This House', which He did.

WAITING FOR THE TIDE TO GO OUT

In contrast to our winter visits to Mamam's were the high-summer ones, when our tireless aunt, having made the beds, emptied the chamberpots, cooked us breakfast and packed picnic baskets, would round us up for the long walk down to the promenade and the beach, there to spend the whole day paddling and building sandcastles, our skin radiant from the sun's golden touch – building us up for the winter, our aunt called it. The street leading to the promenade seemed to end in the blue sky, luminous and endless.

Our excitement mounted until we were nearly sick – would the tide be in or out? Should it turn out to be the former, our spirits sank with a thud and patience had to be exerted. Meanwhile, we'd dangle our legs over the railings and try not to quarrel while our aunt went off round the town with my mother to pass the time.

Eventually, the beautiful and heady scent of newly washed-up seaweed confirmed that the tide was on its way out, leaving grey-white pebbles, then sand, drying out rapidly. Nature's playground spread out before us for our delight.

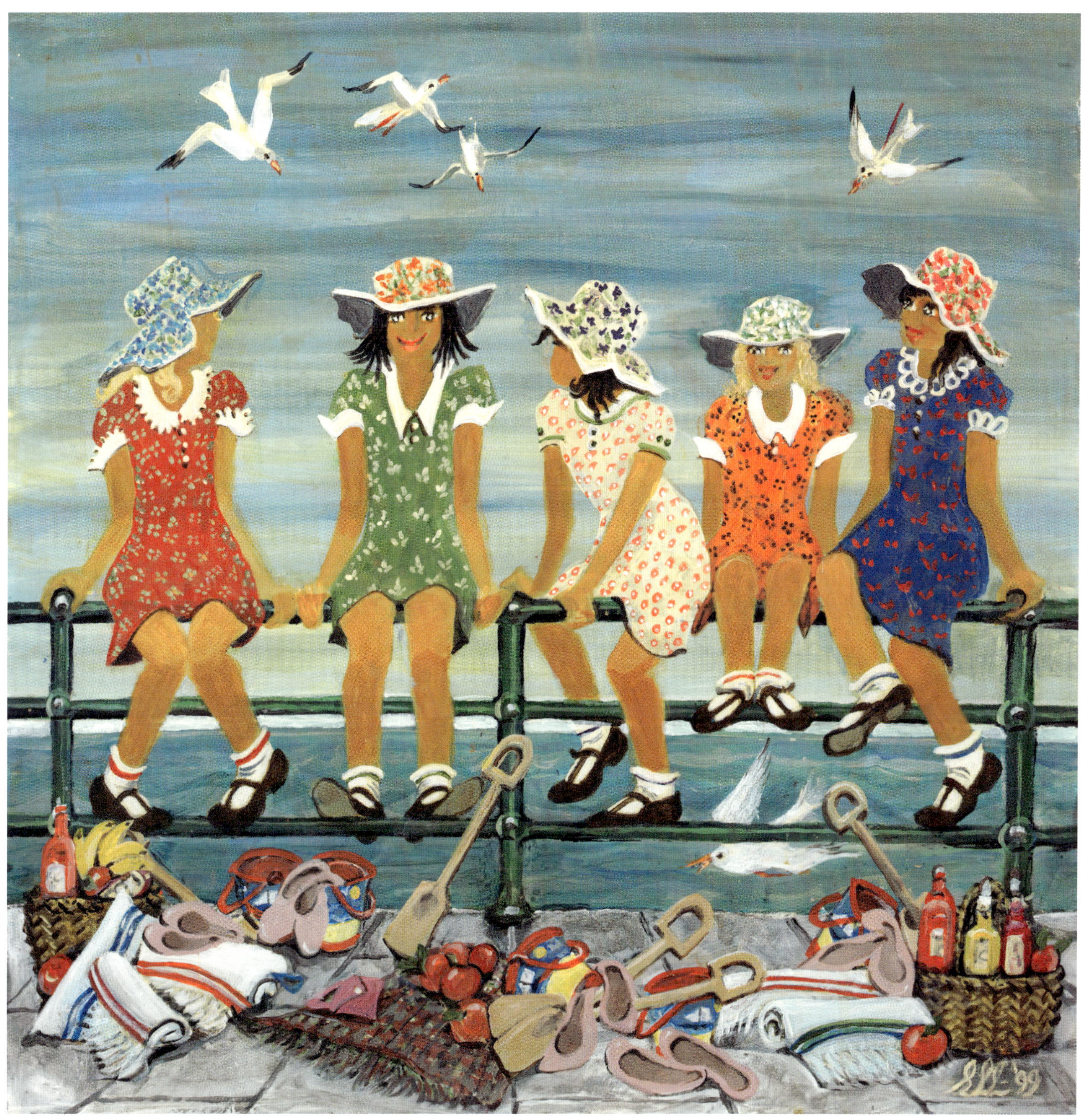

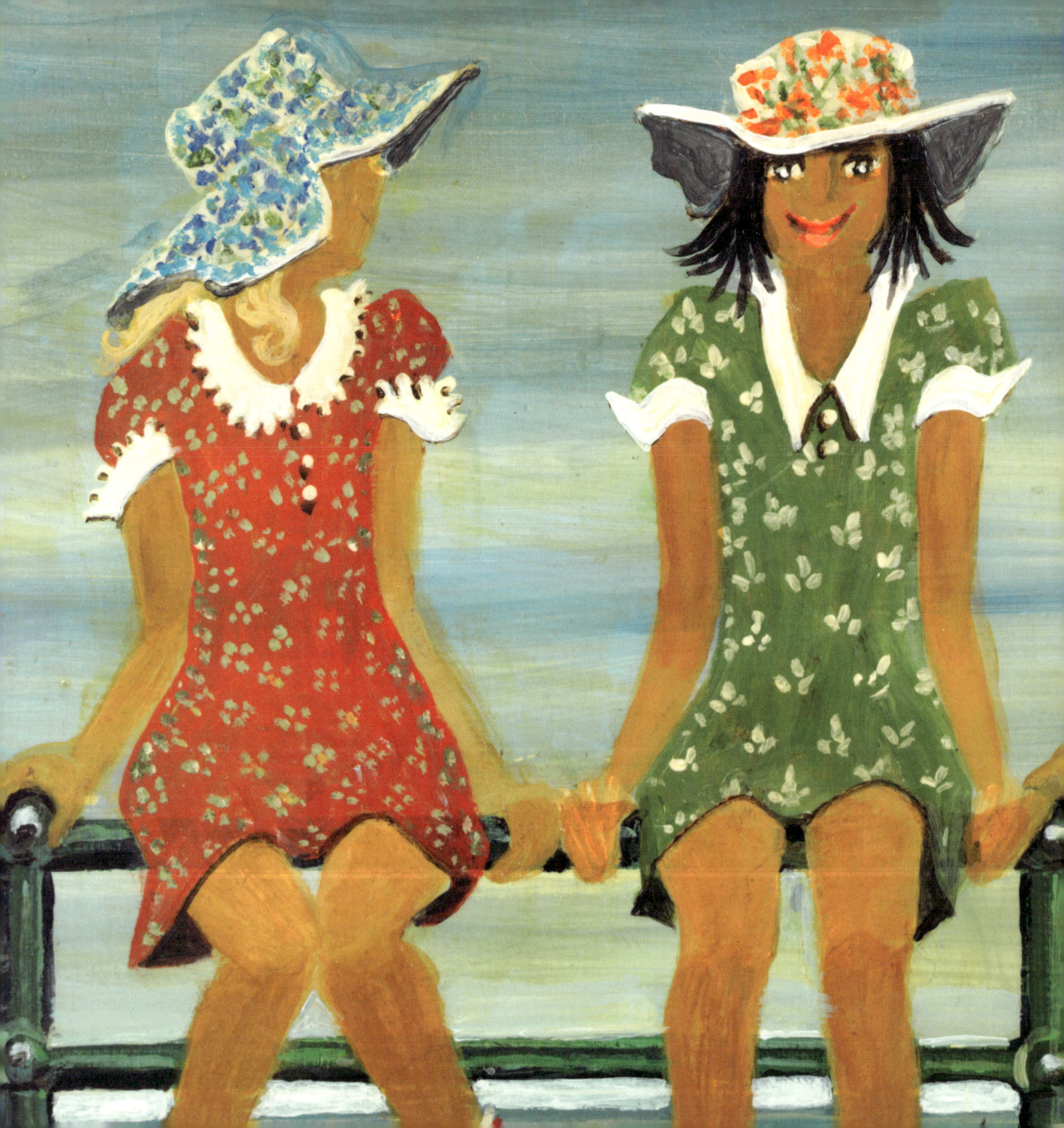

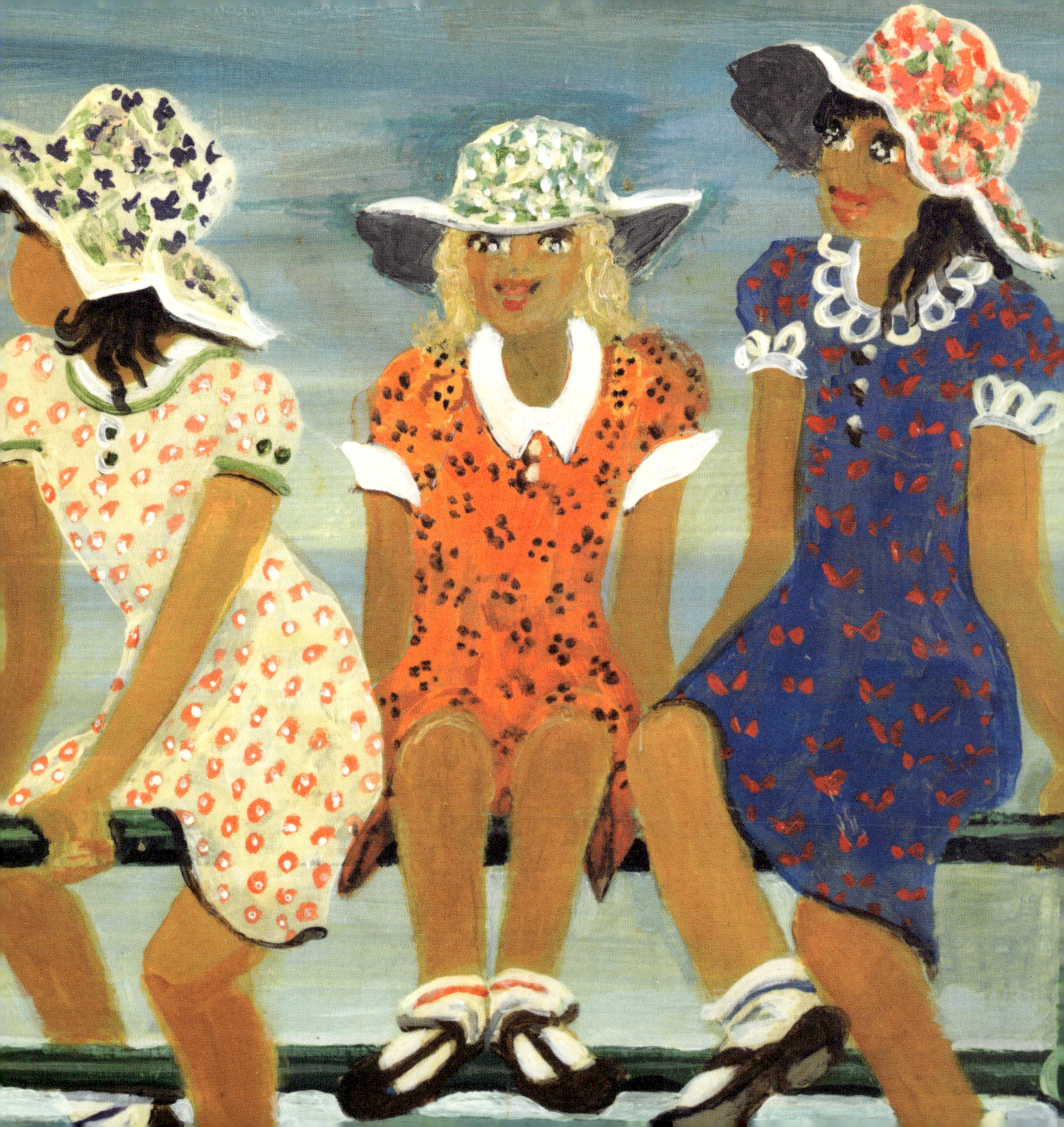

SPRING TIDE

Another wilder seaside outing was to dice with death at the springtide, again taken there by the tireless indulgent aunt who ascribed that oceanic phenomenon to Earth tipping over now and again, swilling the oceans about. Our particular patch of ocean swilled miles up into the air once it hit the promenade wall, towering over our heads as we stood waiting beneath the wave as gravity took over and down crashed a deluge, right on top of our waiting heads. The competition was to see who could stick it out the longest before having to run for our lives in the opposite direction, screaming and shouting and drenched to the skin. Meanwhile, our aunt sat patiently in the shelter, sucking boiled sweets and staring at nothing, having a nice rest.

Eventually, bedraggled as drowned rats, we clustered, shivering plaintively around her, pleading to go home. Out came her worn leather black purse and off to the taxi rank we went for a fast ride home, the children with just enough energy left to fight for the little backwards seats which folded down. Once home, it was into pyjamas and down again to the roaring coal fire in the living room, there to toast bread spiked onto a long brass fork, the fierce heat doing the bread to a turn, butter and jam knifed on quickly and consumed even faster. Then it was off to bed, to sleep like the dead.

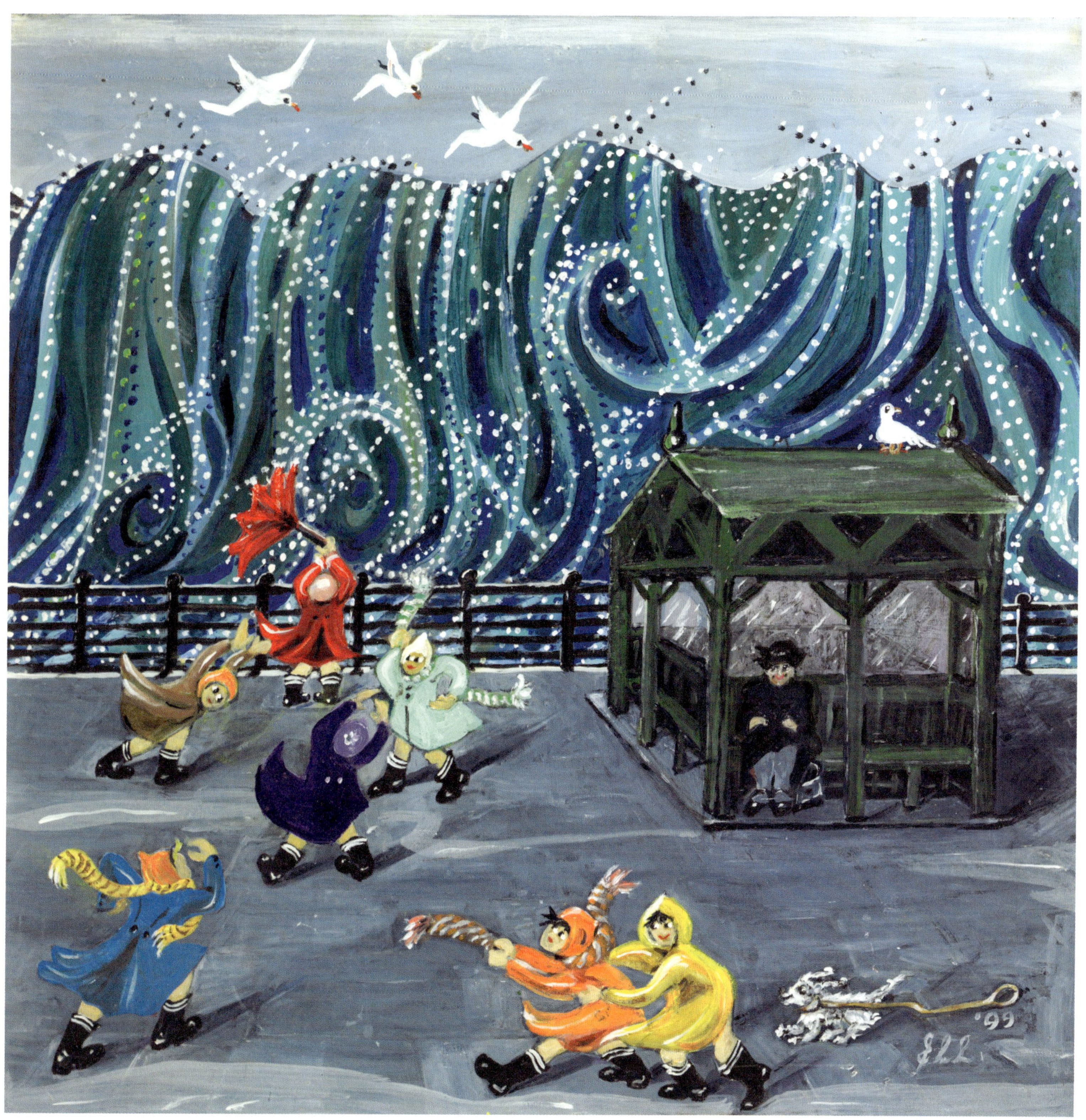

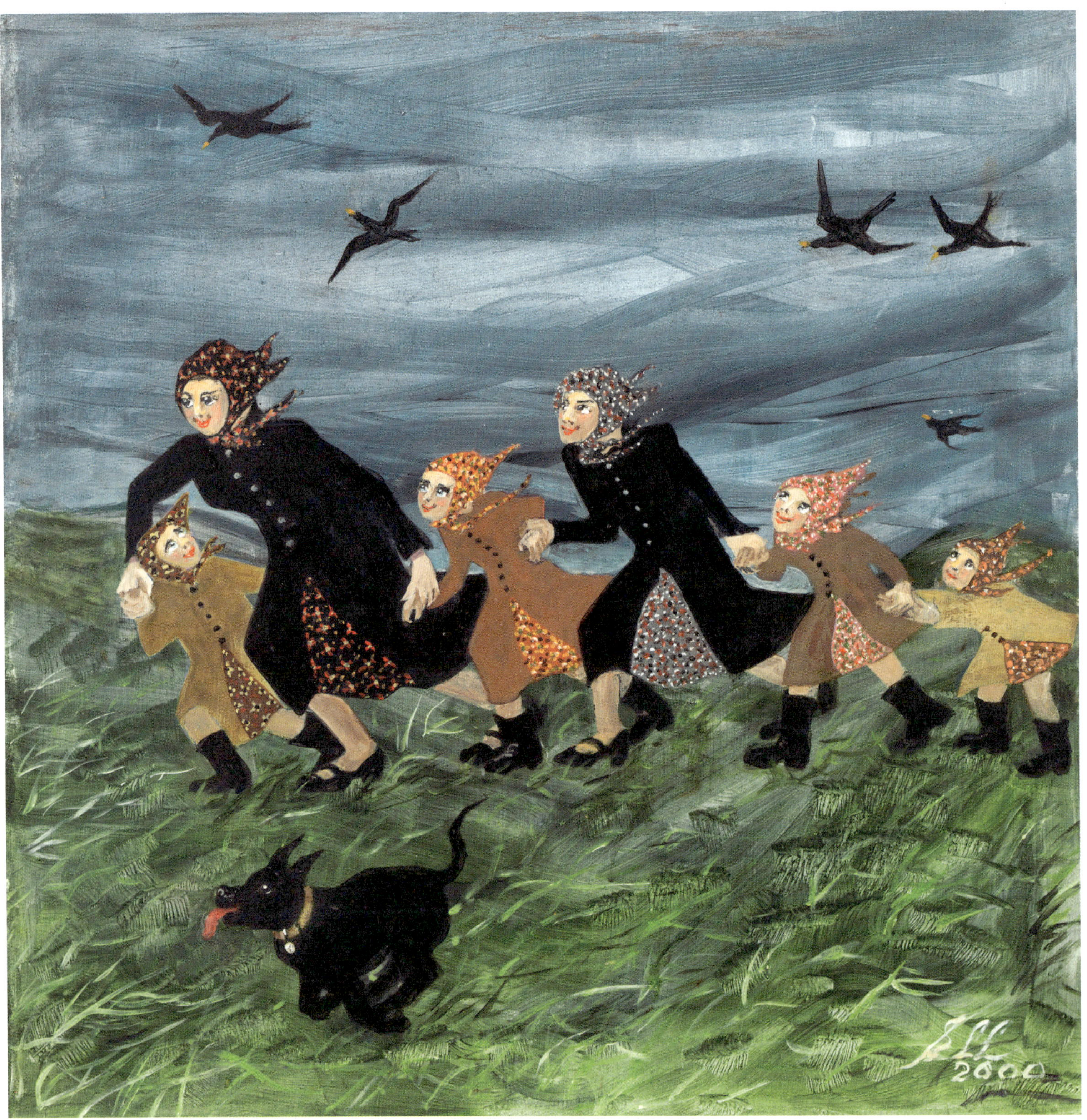

BLOWING AWAY THE COBWEBS

There was nothing like the coast for blowing cobwebs away in winter after too much sitting and playing indoors because of bad weather. The lofty headland was the place to go, well wrapped up and hand in hand for fear of being blown over by a strong gust of salty drizzle. My aunt's dog had to come too, of course, having lain in the hall for days, chin on paws, waiting. The trick was never to shelter from bad weather in the first place, but to go out and welcome the rain, sleet, wind or snow, the cold, the frost, challenge being the spice of life.

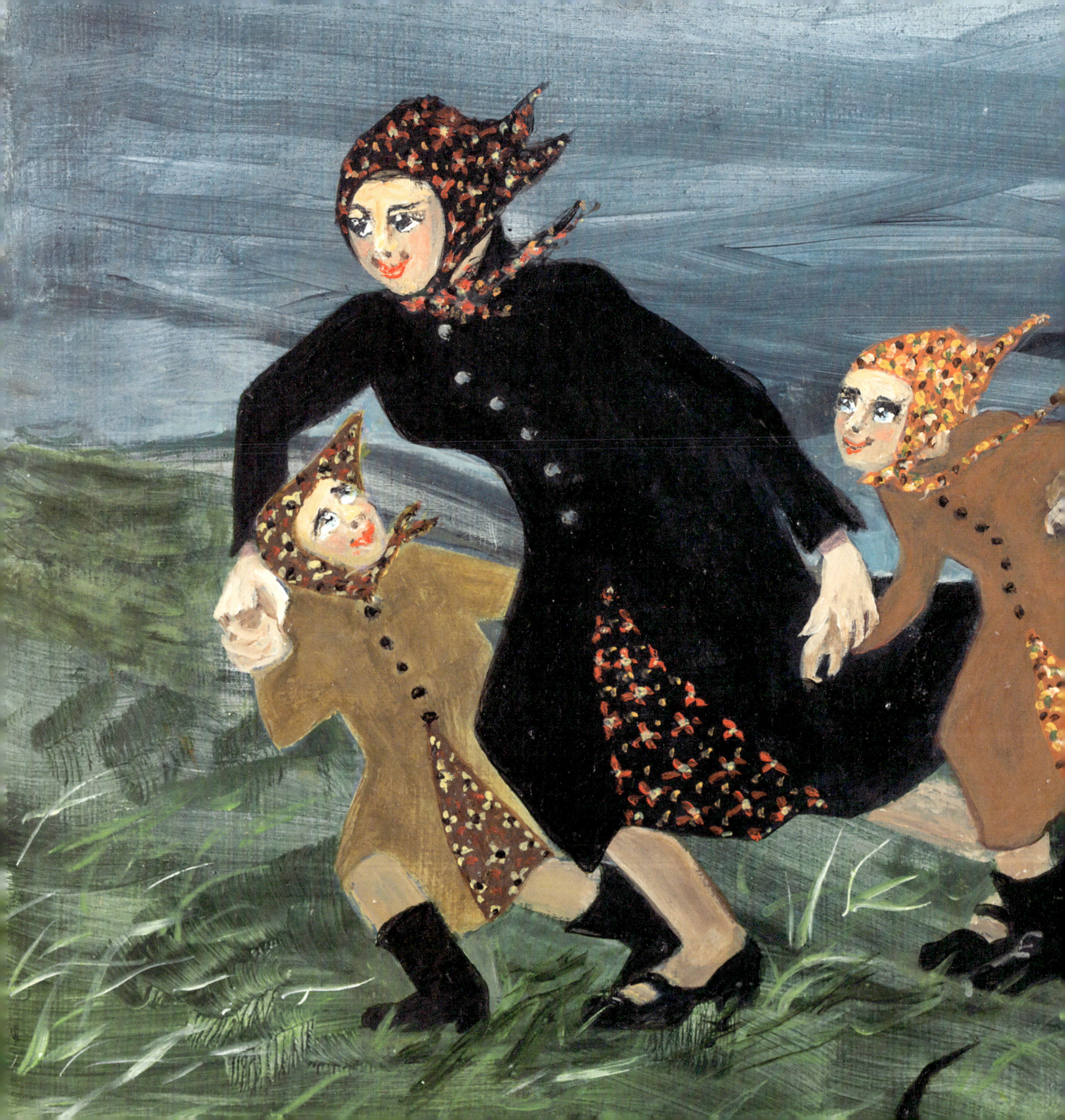

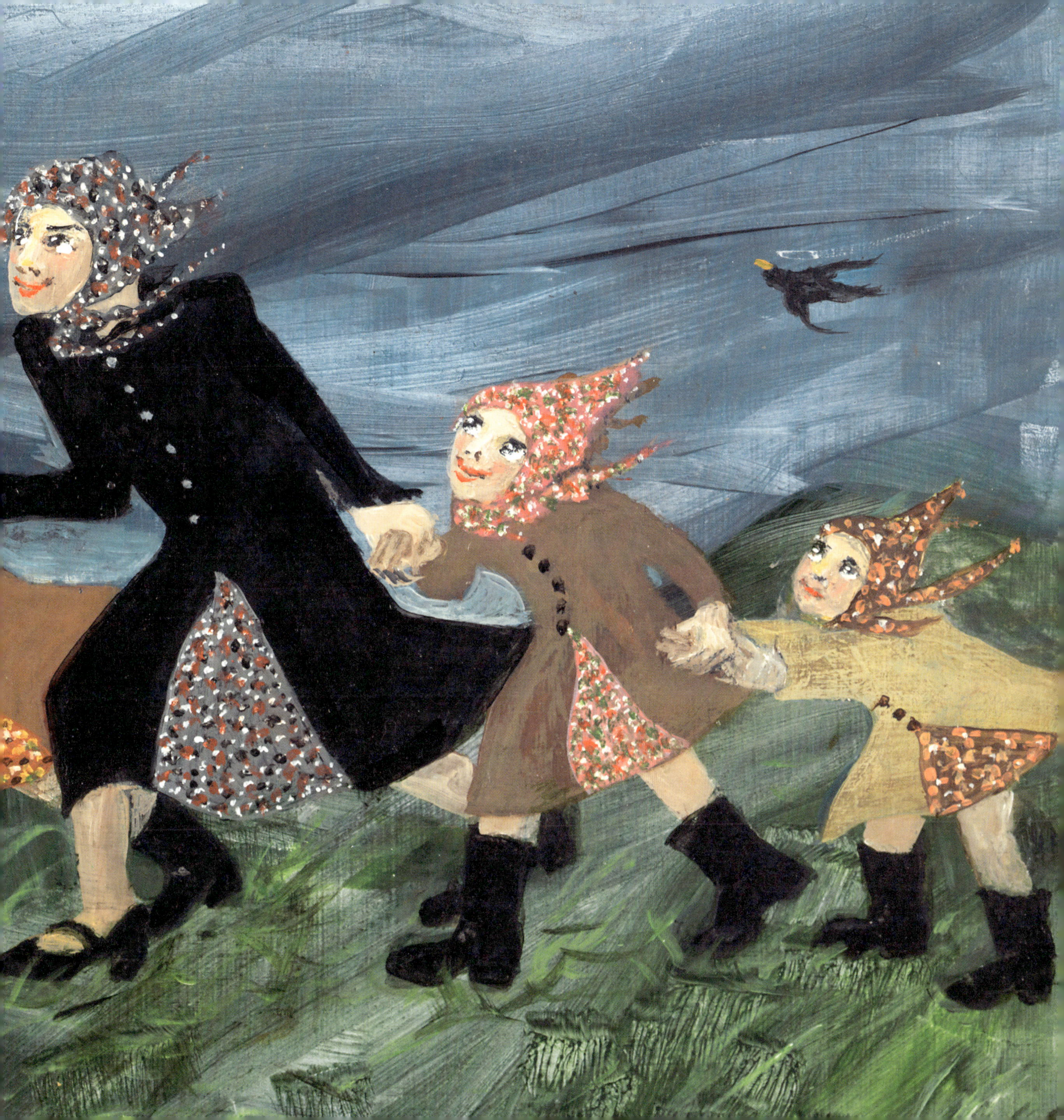

CORONA POP

Under Mamam's stairs was a hidden treasure: four bottles of Corona pop – raspberry, lemon, dandelion and burdock and orange. A boy on a tricycle used to deliver it, stacked in a metal basket fixed to the back. A loud bell on the handlebars alerted customers to the treat in store for them. The fizzy pop, topped by a metal and ceramic lid, was kept under the stairs because of its icy-cold stone-slabbed floor. Nothing else was kept there, and only my aunt was allowed to open it and distribute the contents.

The painting depicts an assorted crowd of cousins, tongues hanging out after a hot day on the beach, exercising self-control whilst the cupboard door was unlocked and a bottle selected. Glasses were ceremoniously filled as though with the best champagne, with orders to sip slowly. Such bliss to the tastebuds, and balm to dry throats, followed by stifled burps and apologies as gas was regurgitated from stomachs. That was the best pop I ever tasted in my life.

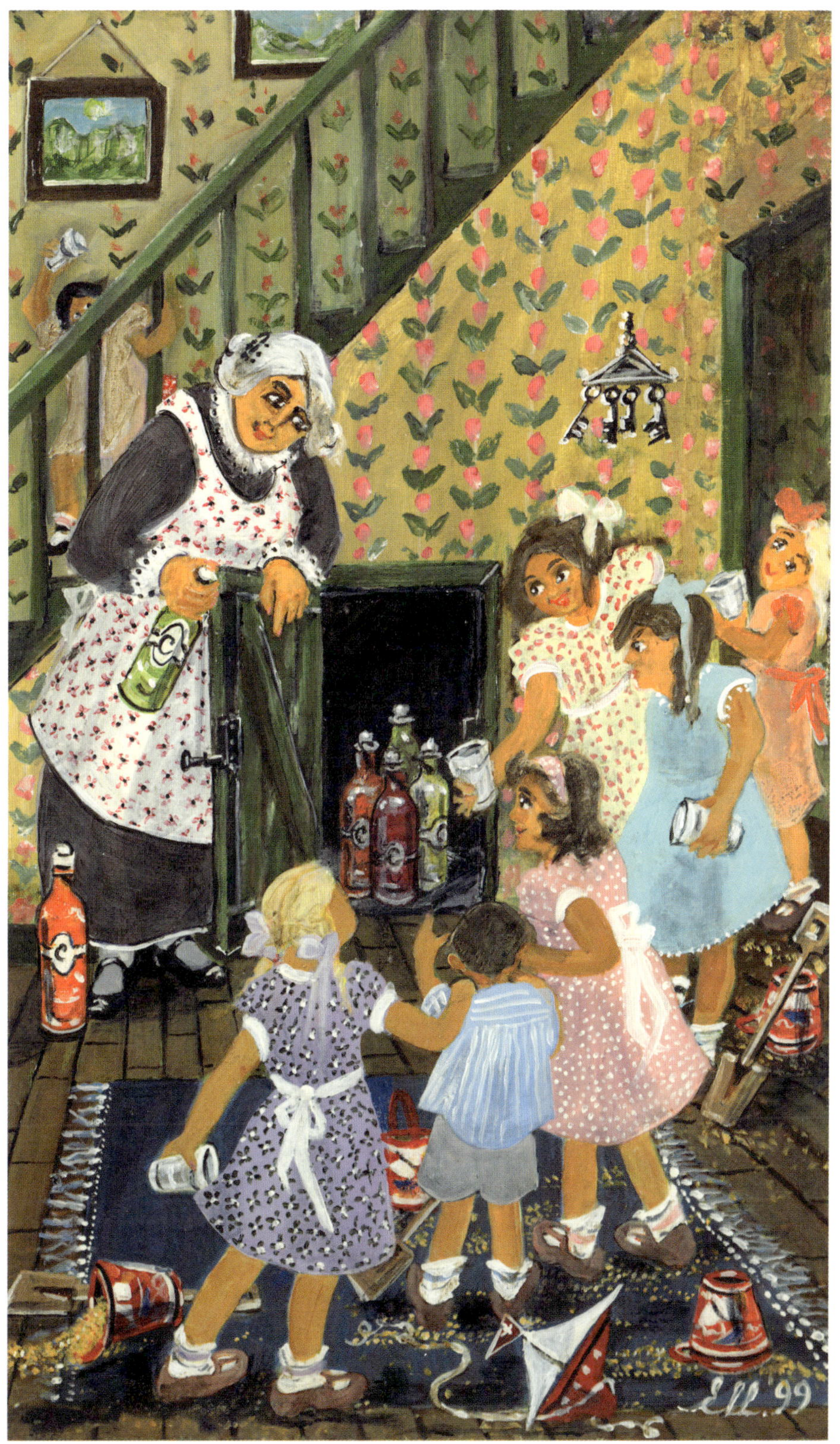

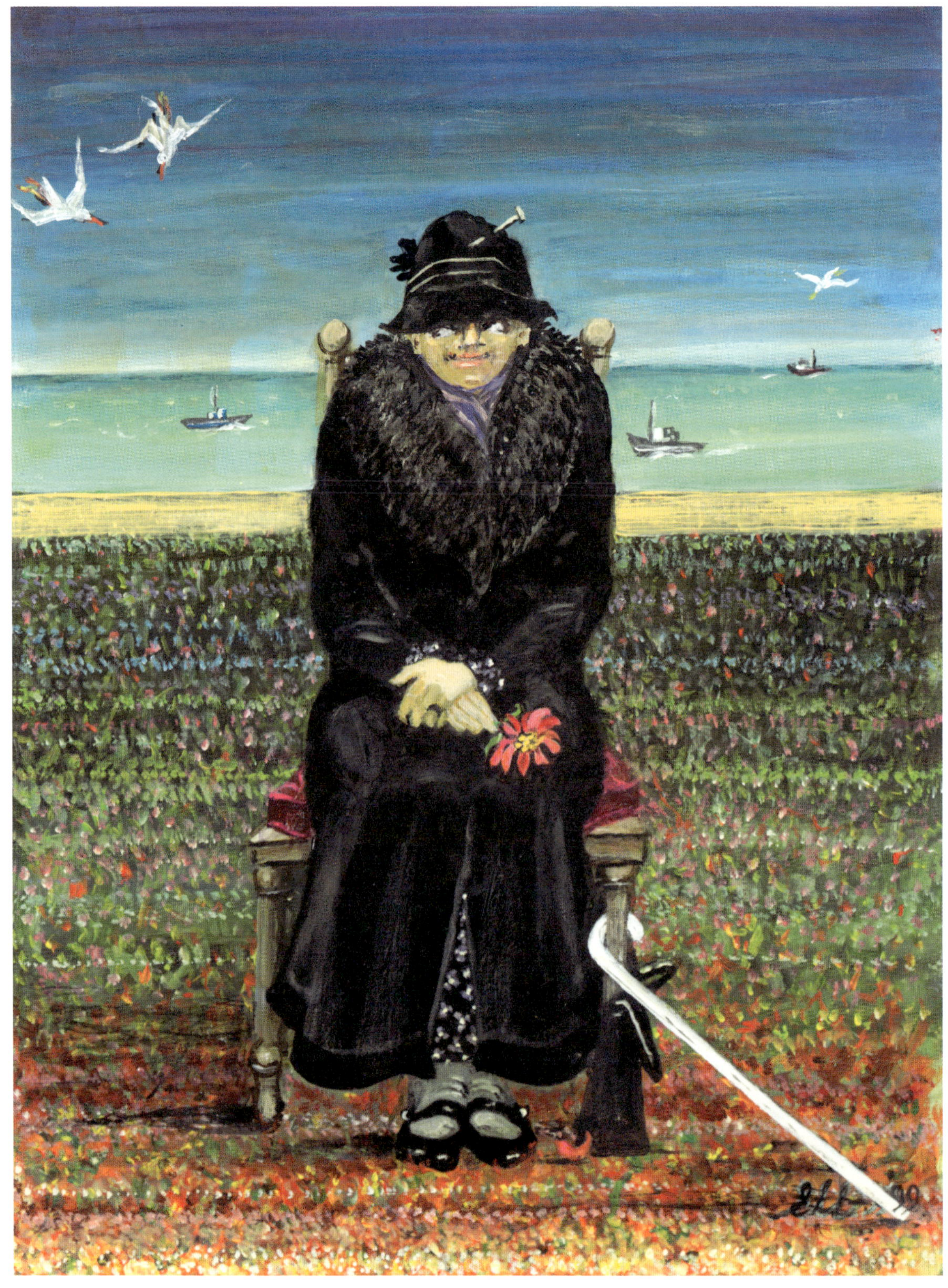

MAMAM 'SEEING'

This is Mamam, my mother's mother, a quiet, gentle lady, tiny in stature, who produced eight children in her early years, a few of them as an immigrant to America's Midwest. I hardly ever heard her speak, and then it was softly. I do not know whether she ever saw me, her granddaughter, because I can't remember when she first went blind from cataracts, and I suspect she may have been deaf too, living in her own gentle world; I could stand right by her and she gave no sign of knowing that. It was disquieting and also sad – I could not reach her even though I yearned to. She also always kept her worn and delicate hands firmly folded in her lap.

THE GHOST OF AUNTY NELLIE

This painting continues the theme of loss, the subject being my beloved, merry, generous spinster aunt of the mutilated fingers – Aunty Nellie. I portray her as a ghost, standing in the garden against a background of sea and sky, a newly baked gooseberry tart offered proudly. Her baking was delicious, and when my father drove us north-west over the mountains to stay with in CNY 616, our car, I swore I could smell her lamb and mint sauce dinner from there. She loved me to tell her that, proclaiming that her culinary skills were all due to advice from a French sea captain she nearly married once.

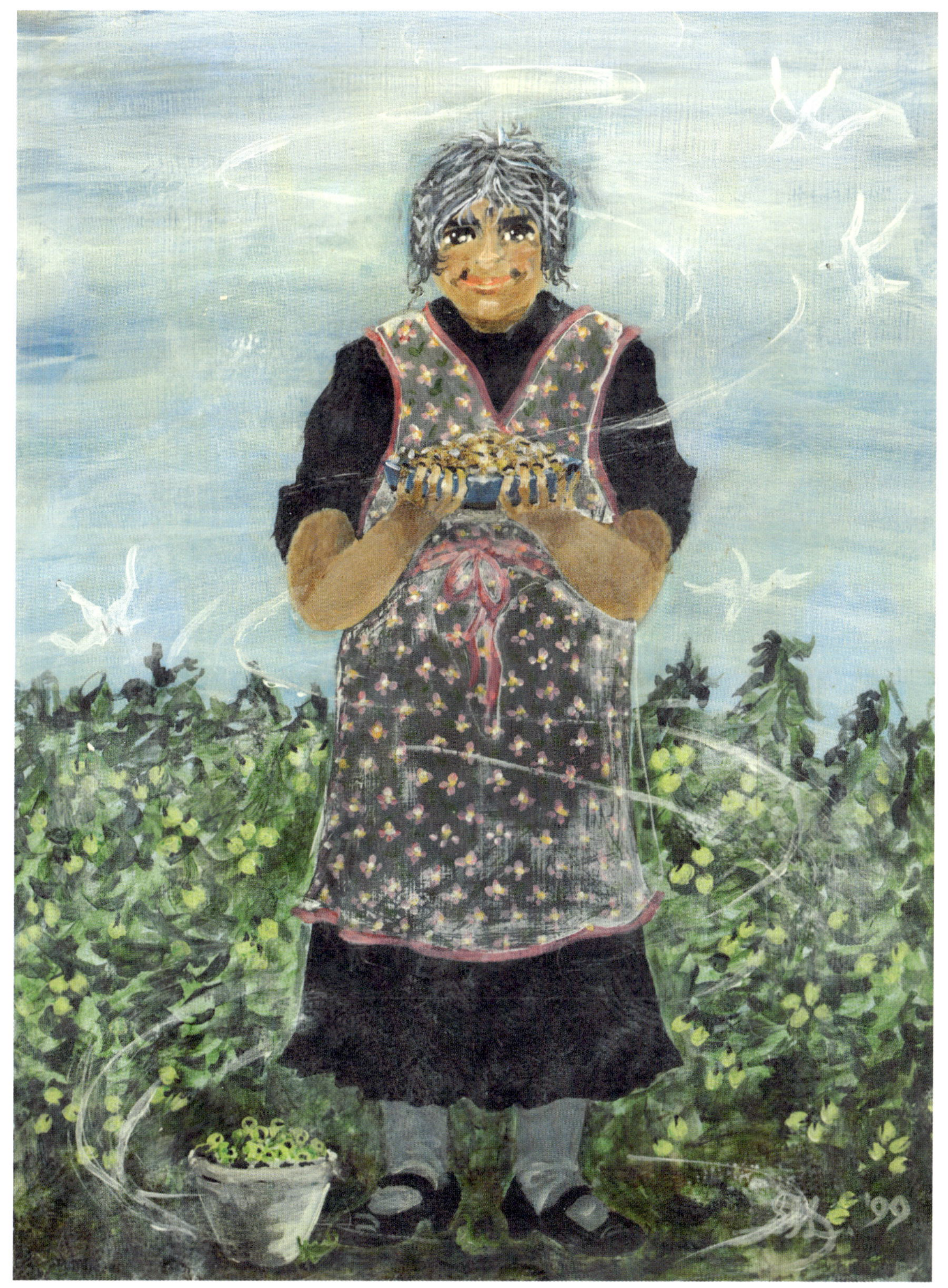

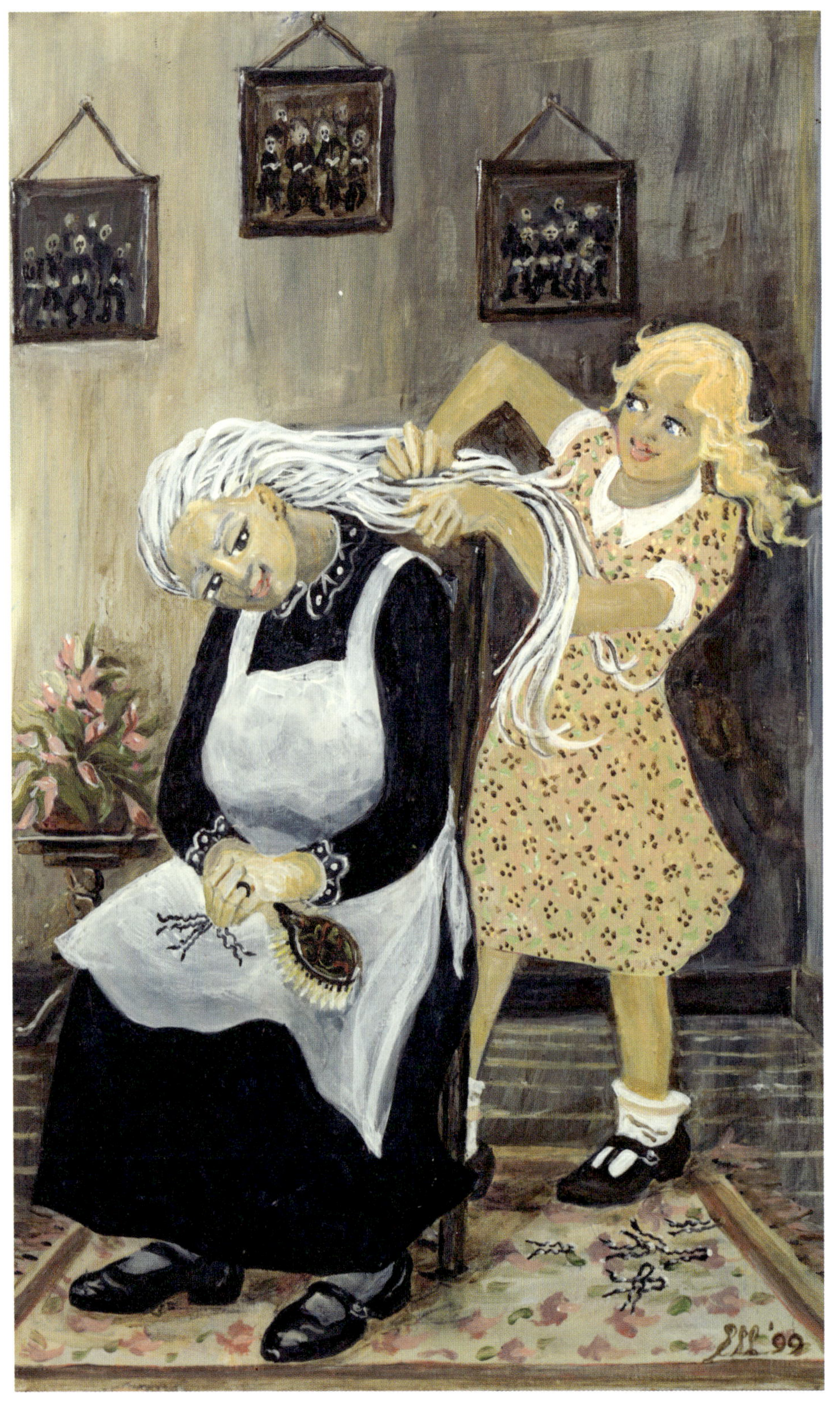

BINDING HER HAIR

Hair figured largely in our lives. This painting depicts me trying to tame a relative's hair which was long and fine. The aim was to pin it into 'earphones', two plaited lengths coiled round and round over each ear, an impossible challenge for me which caused great amusement to the victim.

RAGS FOR CURLS

Occasionally, my mother would inadvertently cause me excruciating discomfort by tying rags in my hair in very tight knots to be slept in overnight, the morning unveiling curls all over, to look like Shirley Temple.

I didn't like curls, and I think it was my mother who longed for them, her own hair being fine and straight and, sadly, damaged by too many years of hot curling tongs being administered and heated over a gas flame on the cooker.

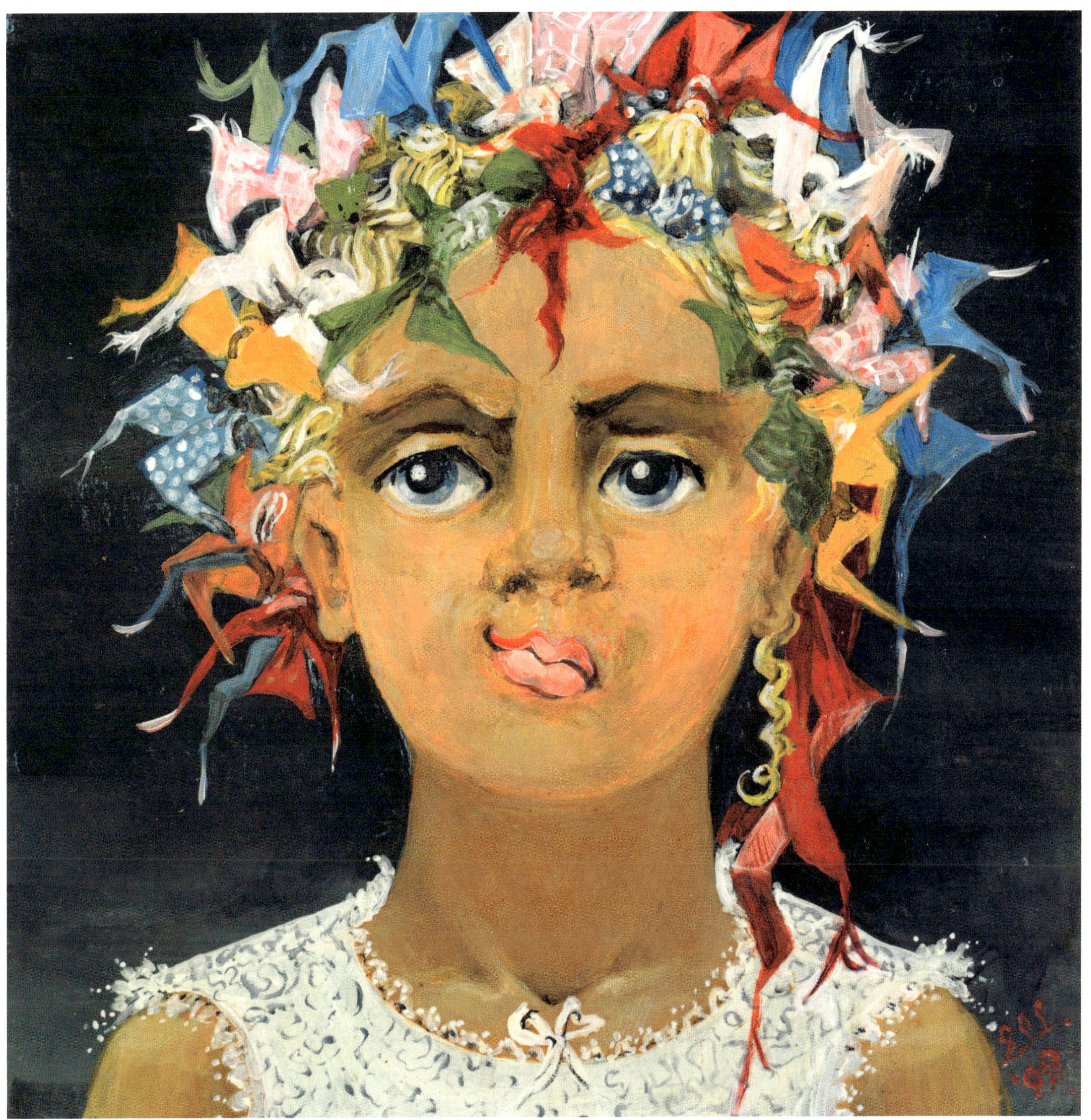

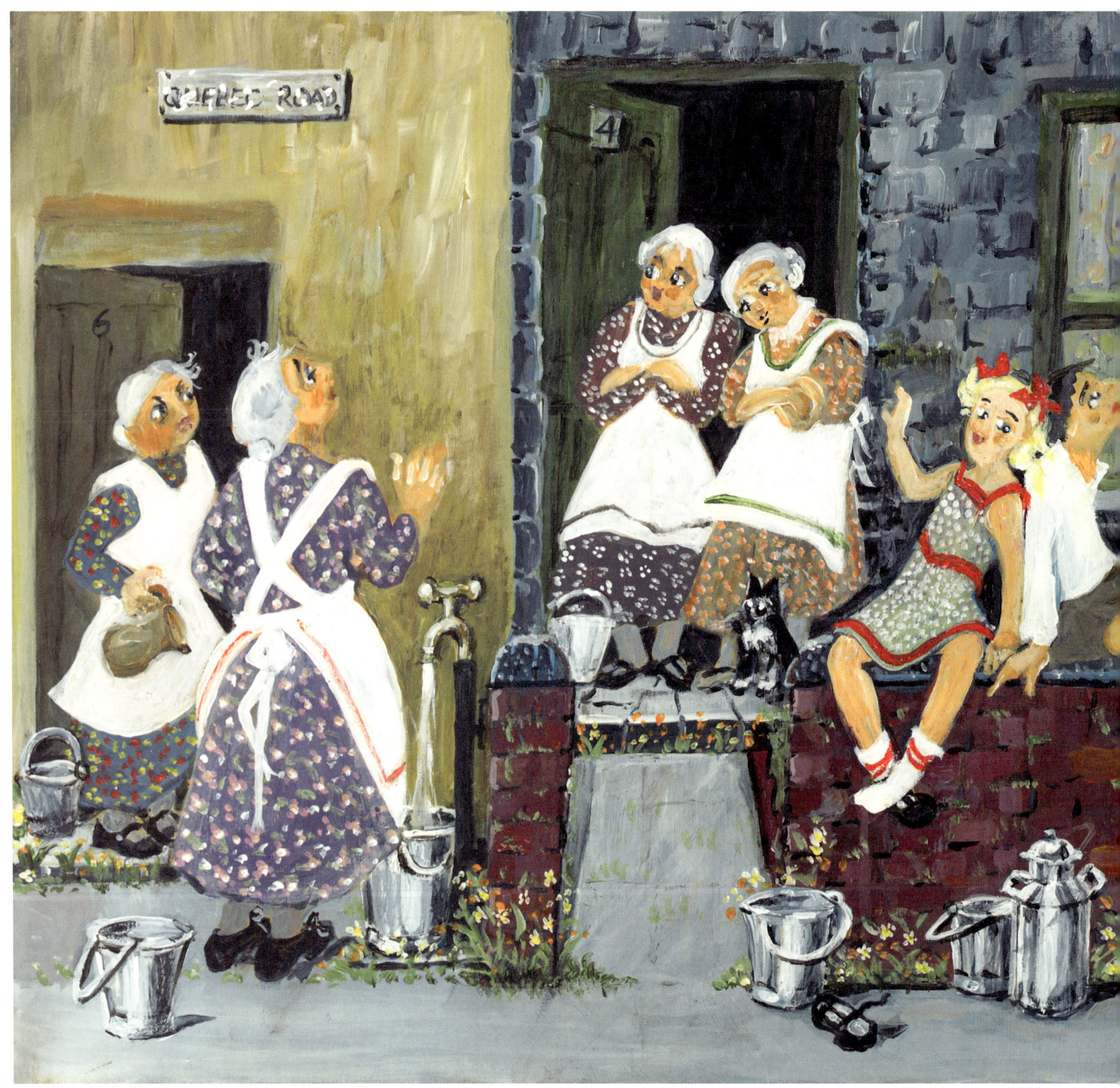
JUBILEE ROAD

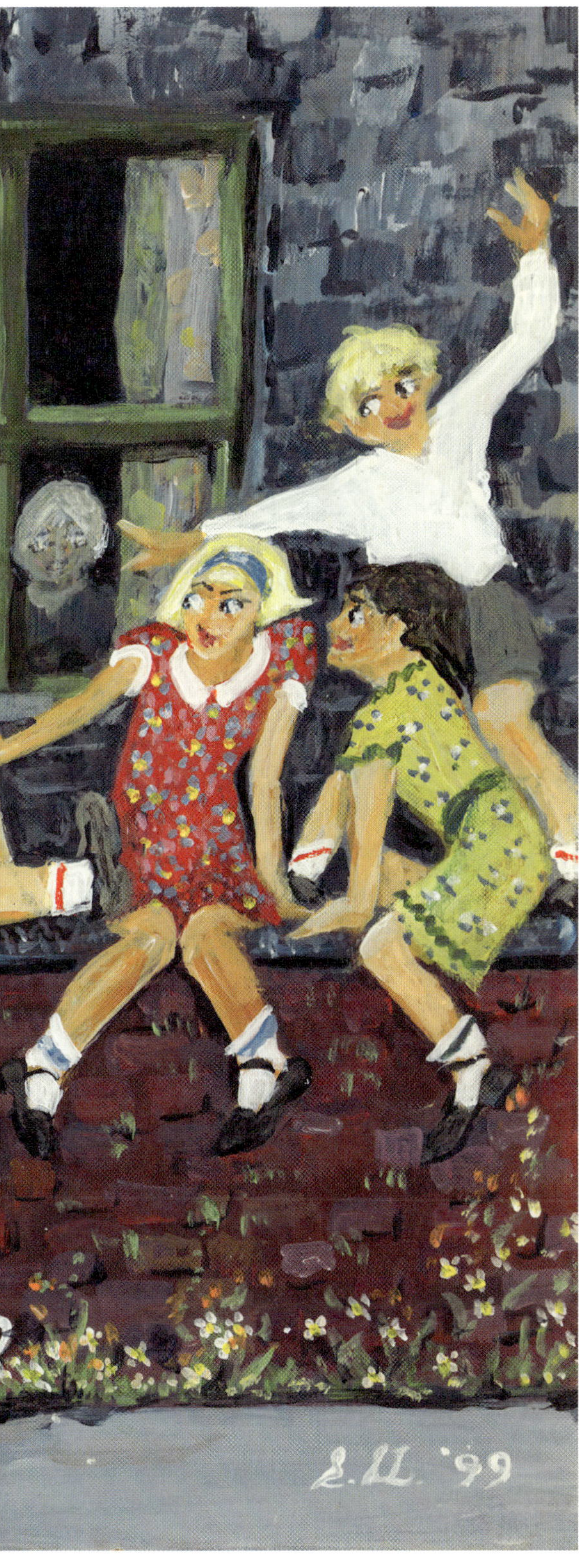

COMMUNAL TAP

As I look at this painting I can actually feel the smooth texture of the burnished blue stone capping topping the wall outside Mamam's house. It might have been called Staffordshire Blue, and being curved it made a wonderful seat for us children as we waited in the queue to get water from the communal tap outside, a domestic chore we fought over. With the boys preferring to tussle and perform acrobatics, we girls just sat swinging our legs and being good. The communal tap was a truly tribal watering hole, the women chattering and exchanging news, occasionally gossiping about someone, but always polite and waiting their proper turn. When our turn came we obeyed strict instructions not to waste a drop, nor to spill any as we carried the full containers down the shiny, polished linoleum floor of the passageway leading to the scullery, far at the back of the house. Turning on the tap took two hands, and when it came the water charged out full force, so you had to be quick to turn it off again, sandalled feet astride the drain and running the gauntlet of giant spiders living there, the boys being busy inventing the story that spiders were crawling up the backs of our legs. Water was brought in twice a day, early morning and early evening.

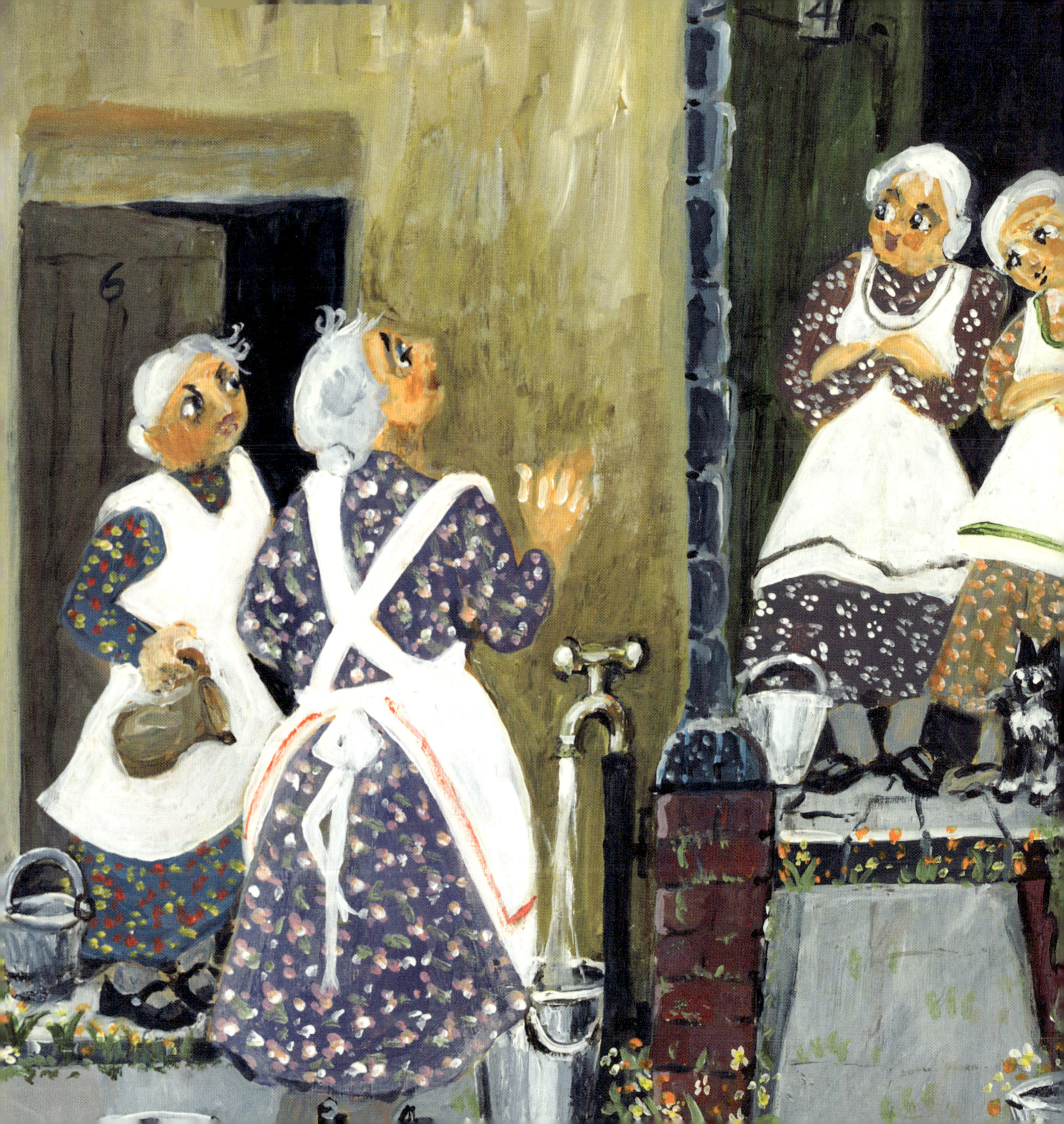

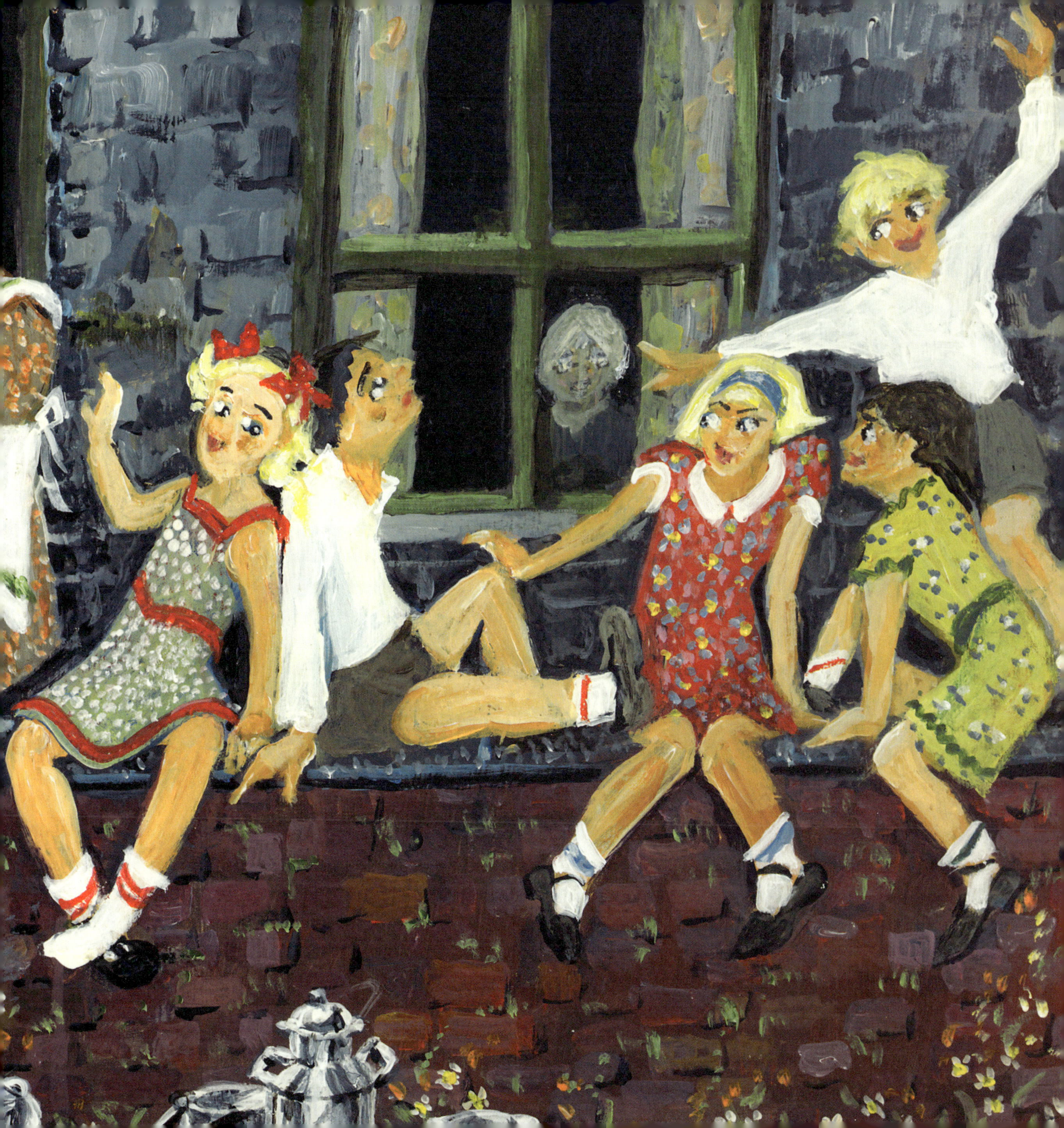

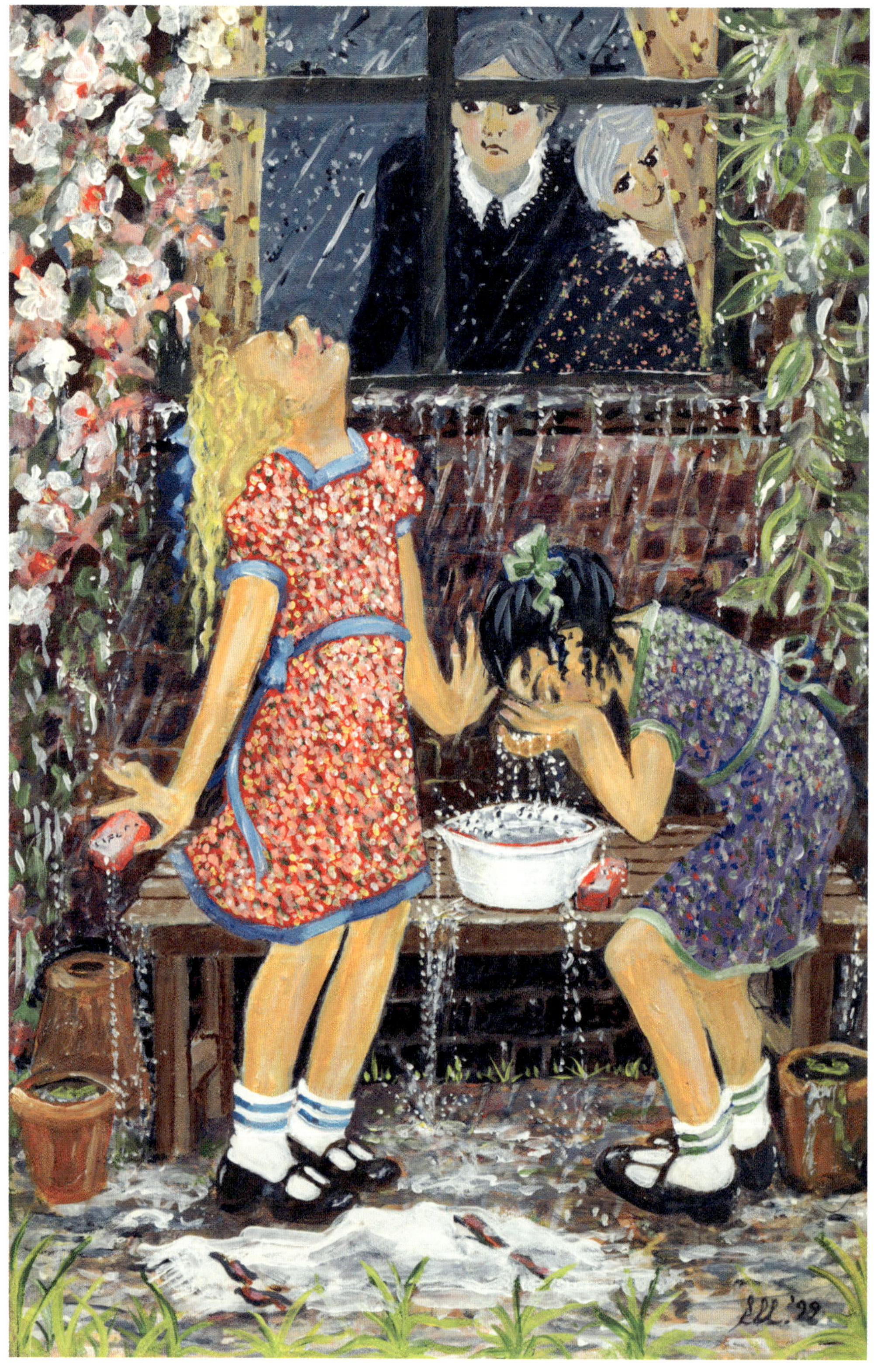

WASHING IN THE RAIN

Growing up in 1930s Wales, there was no bathroom at that time, so washing was done from flowered china basins or white enamelled pans with a coloured rim, red or blue. Soap was red carbolic, perhaps Lifebouy, and thick white towels were aplenty, their dazzling appearance obtained by boiling them in the copper boiler in the scullery and then pegging them out on the long garden line with its old branch for a prop. Sheets were likewise, their exquisite scent of the sea picked up from stiff breezes guaranteed to dry anything in record time. Our aunt was very strict about cleanliness, keeping a white enamel bowl, red soap and fresh towel stationed permanently on a small bench. In summer these were placed outside in the tiny red-cobbled backyard, so that instead of rinsing our faces in the pan of water we could turn them up to the sky when it rained and have the soap rinsed off that way – much more fun.

TY BACH

The absence of piped running water meant there was no indoor lavatory, bedrooms being serviced by pretty, flowered china chamber pots, emptied at the crack of dawn by some mysterious hand, probably my aunt's. Downstairs it was an altogether different matter, for there was a *ty bach* (Welsh for little house) out in the back garden, equipped to deal with nature's call in an efficient and hygienic way, albeit primitive. It involved a wooden bench with a round hole cut in it, into which was lowered a white enamel bucket heavily laced with strong disinfectant. On the wall cut squares of newspaper were hung neatly, spiked onto a long, rusty nail. In the middle of the night, someone took this full receptacle away and tottered down the long earthen path to the cesspit at the very end of the garden.

This was a deep hole in the ground filled with gravel and sand and some even stronger disinfectant. We children were banned from this area, an easy order to obey, especially as it was surrounded by a wall of stinging nettles.

But the *ty bach* itself was clean and quite comfortable, though it required, in order to enter and use, a stiffening of the upper lip, a clenching of the jaw, due to numerous families of spiders making their home there. Admittedly they kept away the wasps and the flies, but they also objected to the intrusion of human users and would actually get on their long legs and run at you, clambering up your clothes or falling on your head. Myself and the little cousin depicted here correspond every once in a while, she living in London now, and I mentioned that *ty bach* of our childhood all those years ago and my painting of it. She'd never forgotten it either and gave her own graphic account of the horrific experience.

There was a proper bathroom later, but I don't ever remember seeing it. The advent of the Second World War put paid to long holidays spent at Mamam's by the sea and in the bosom of the most loving and merry family I have ever known.

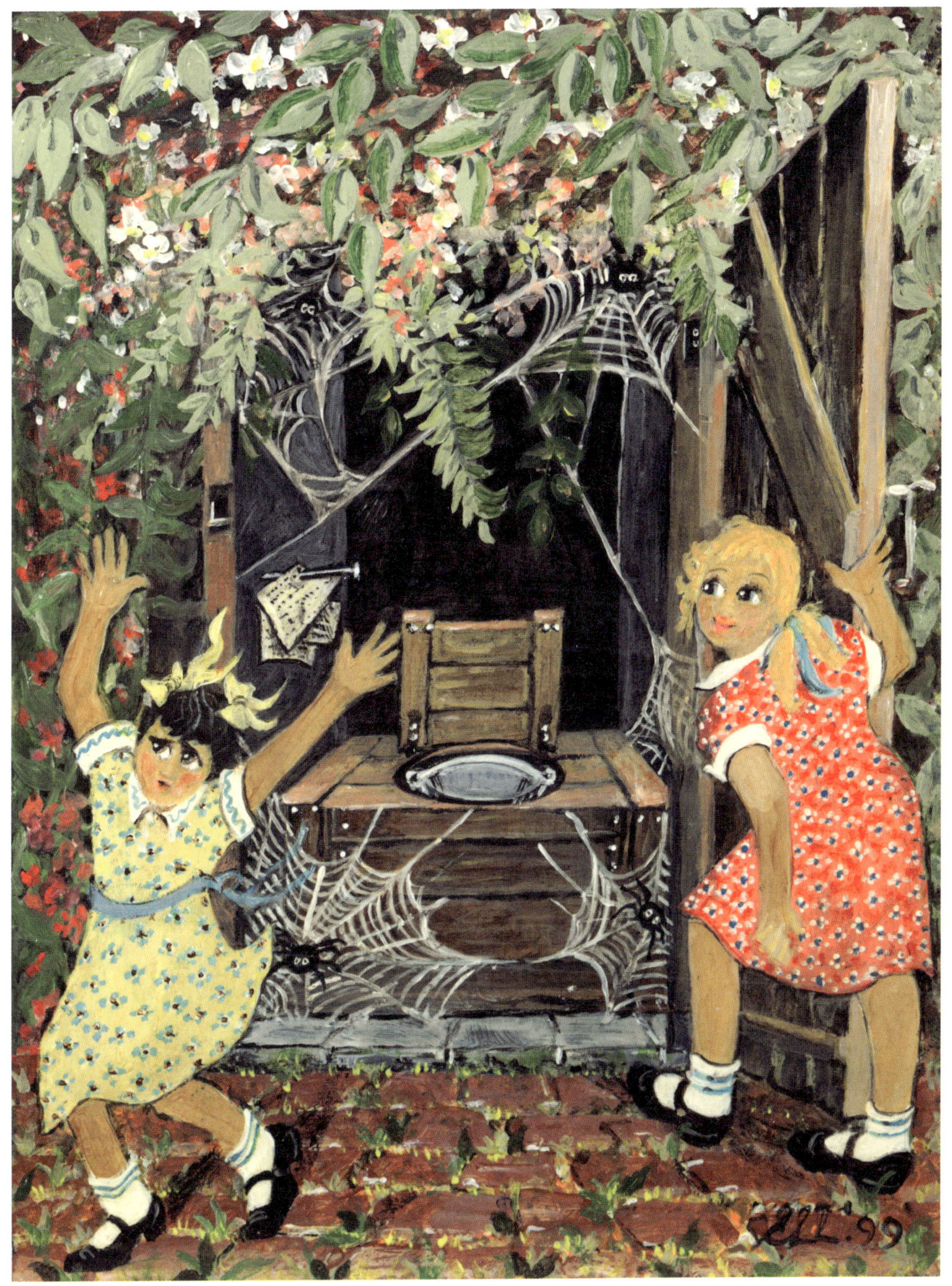

FAIRIES

Our move from the farm to a suburban avenue, with
the consequent availability of girls to play with at
last, instead of boys, meant that I could talk about
fairies without being poked fun at all the time. One
girl at school who lived with her grandmother in town
kept telling me that there were not only fairies at the
bottom of her garden but that she was on intimate
terms with them, and would I like to come and meet
them one day after school? My mother finally gave in to
my excited pleas, so off I went to her house, a terraced
one with a long, narrow garden. I felt so excited
and ran all the way. Down she led me, deep into the
undergrowth and brambles, and then came to a halt,
turned around and said, 'They're not here today.'
This was a terrible disappointment for me, so
convincing was my acquaintance. I had believed her
utterly. So this is a painting to heal that blow.

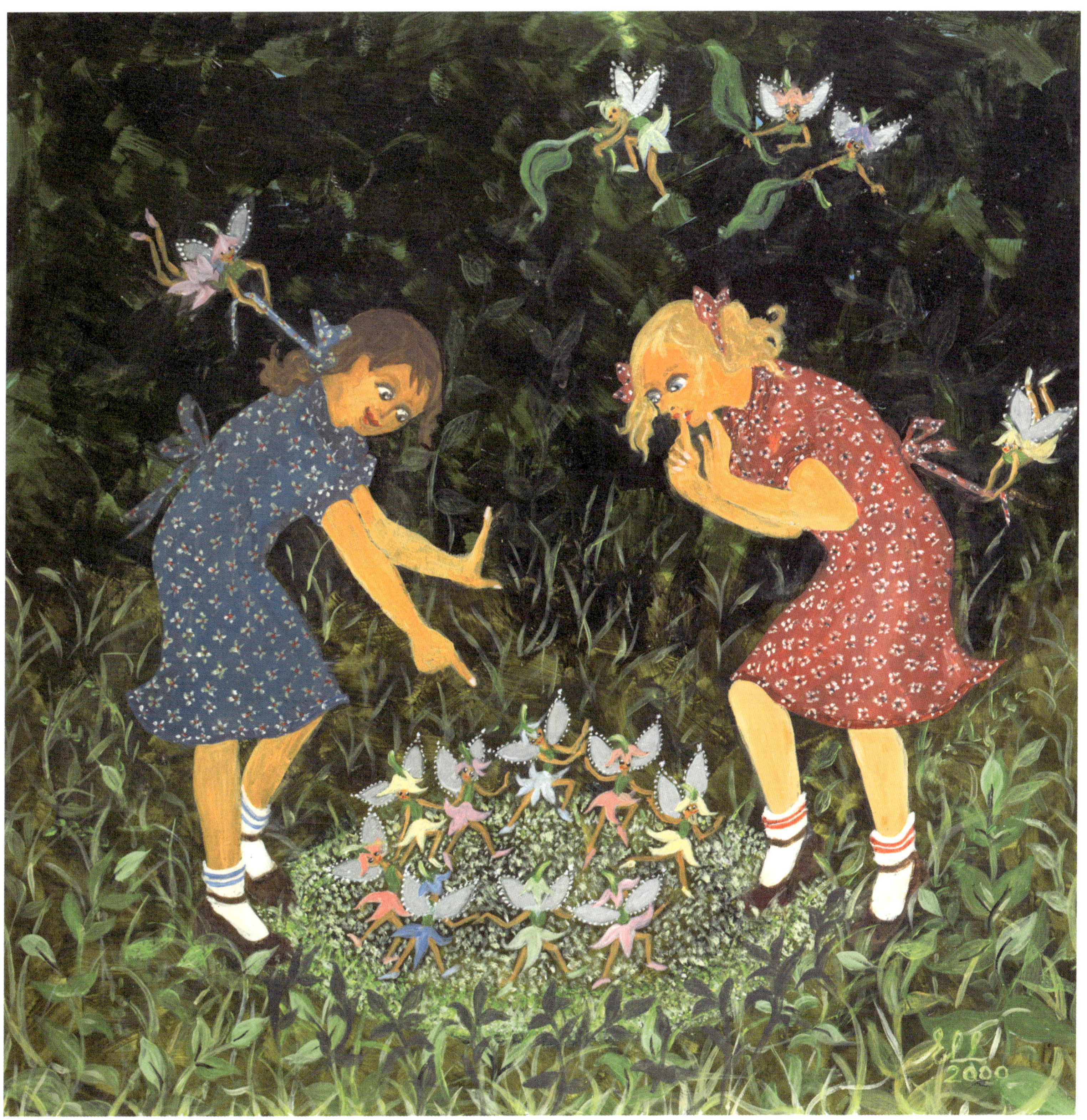

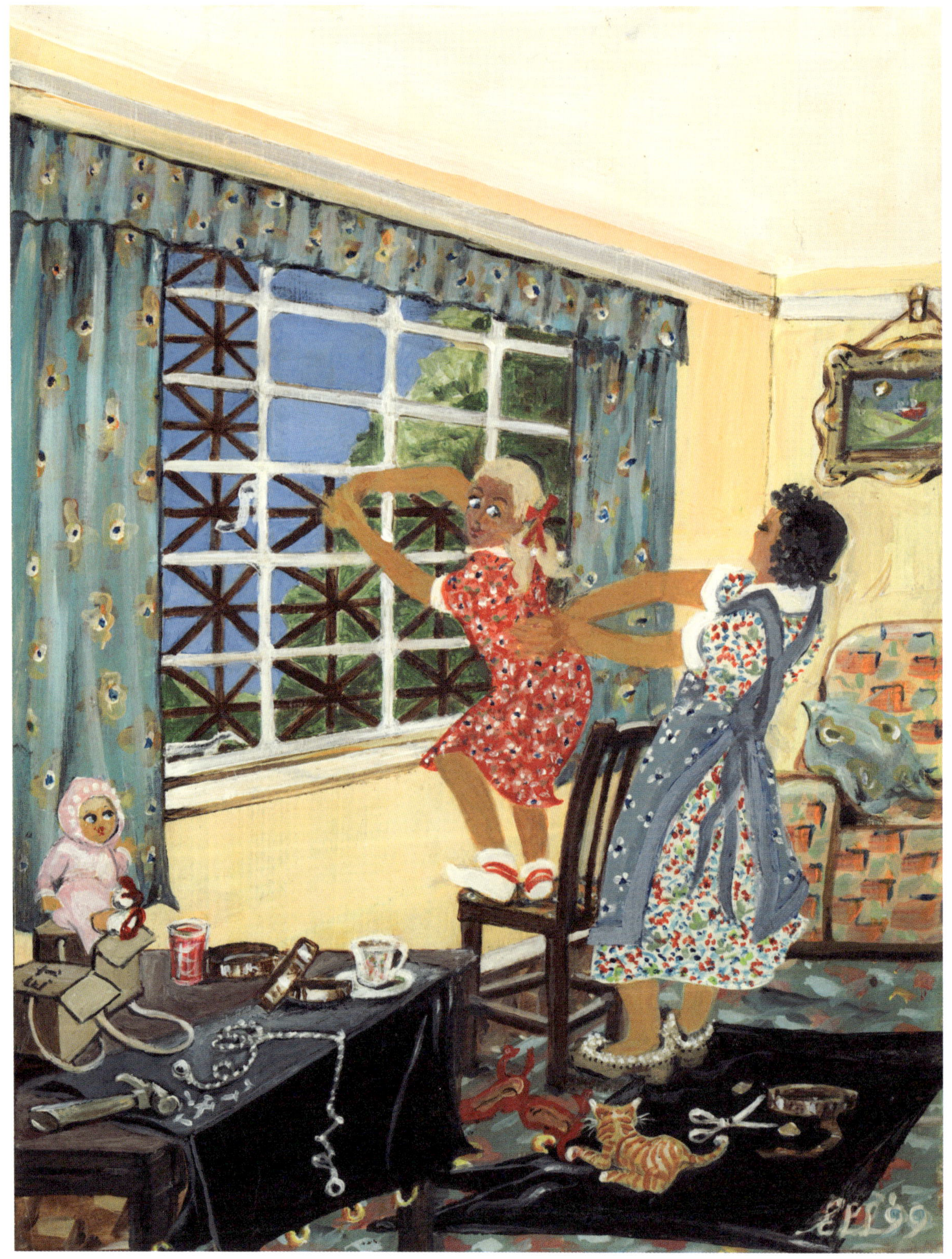

BROWN TAPE FOR WINDOWS

My memory moves to our front room window, and I am helping my mother stick gummed brown paper tape to our windows in pretty patterns with the aim of preventing injury from flying glass, should more bombs fall in the vicinity, that being within a ten-mile radius of important targets – an oil refinery and a steelworks.

BOMB DISPOSAL

The greatest risk to our little part of the world was from bombs being dumped in a fast retreat from the target further west or north to the Midlands then back across the English Channel, our plucky Spitfires in hot pursuit. Quite a lot of dud bombs fell, the army bomb-disposal squads bravely diffusing them before taking them away. Sometimes these 'duds' blew up, killing or maiming the men, who were extremely brave and generally unsung heroes, it was said.

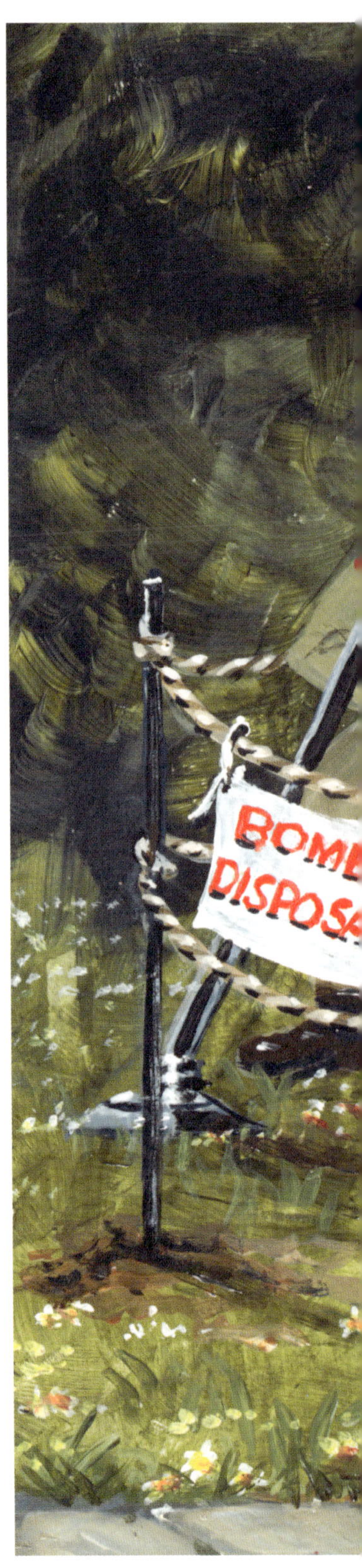

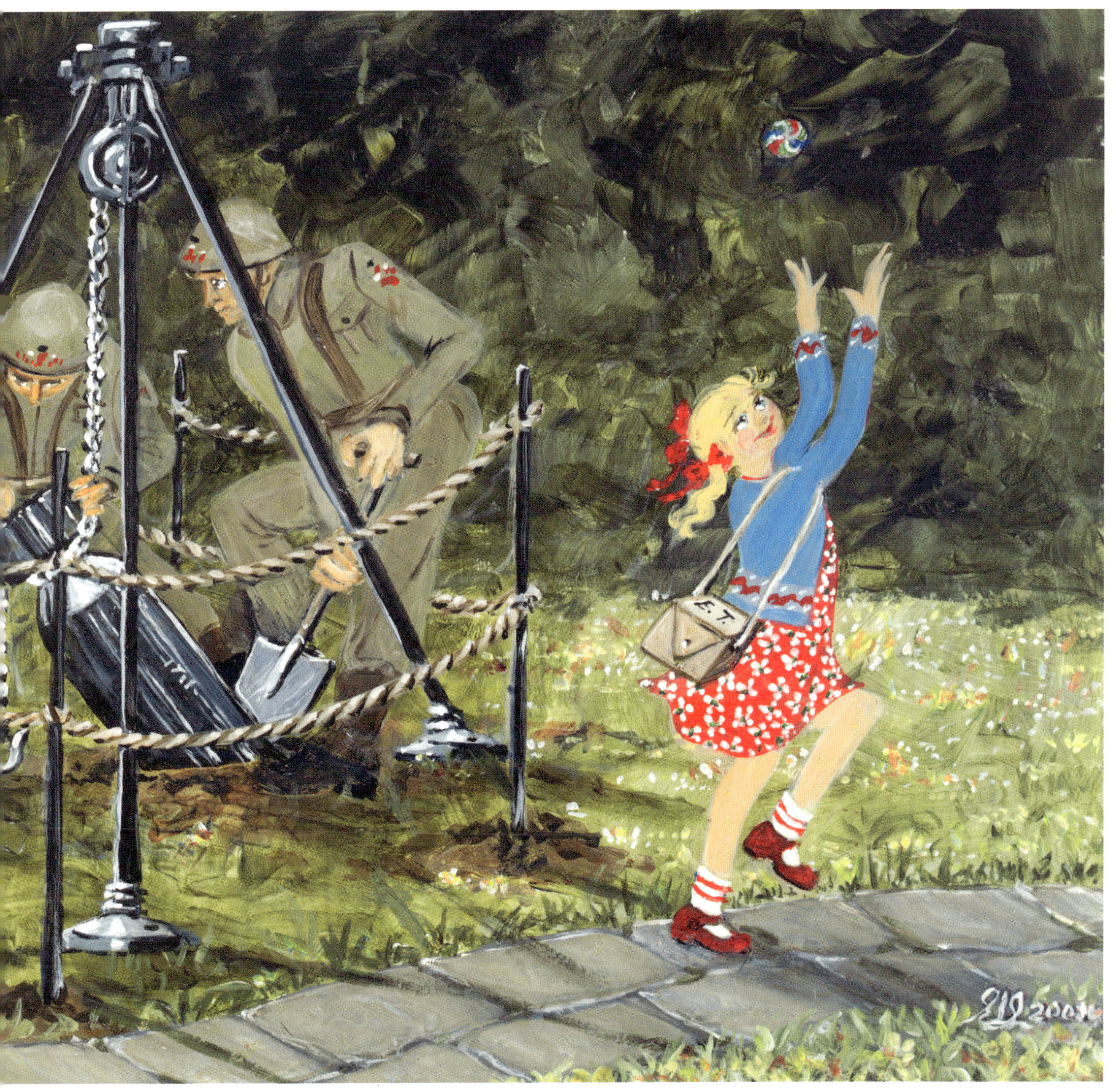

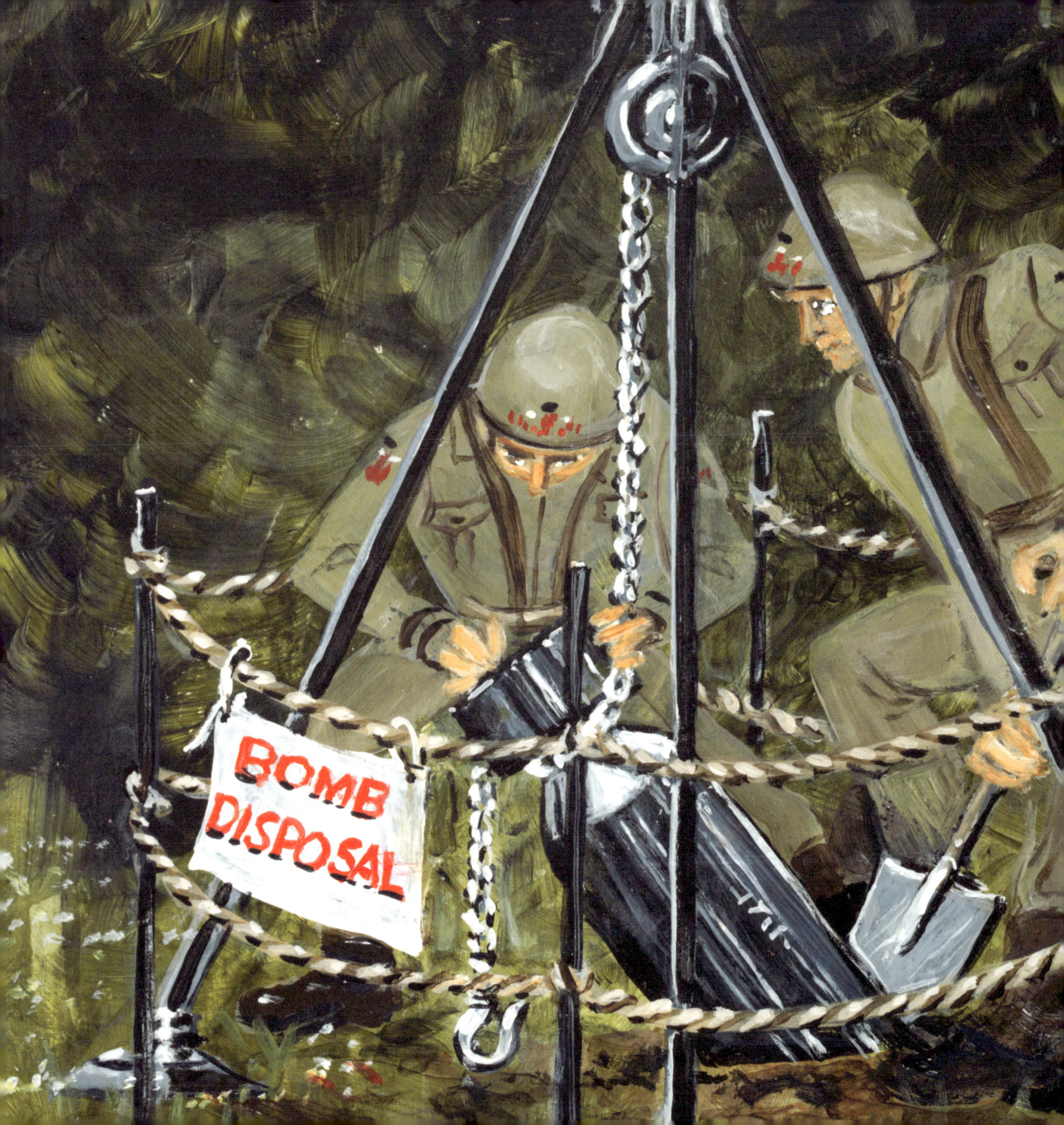
BOMB
DISPOSAL

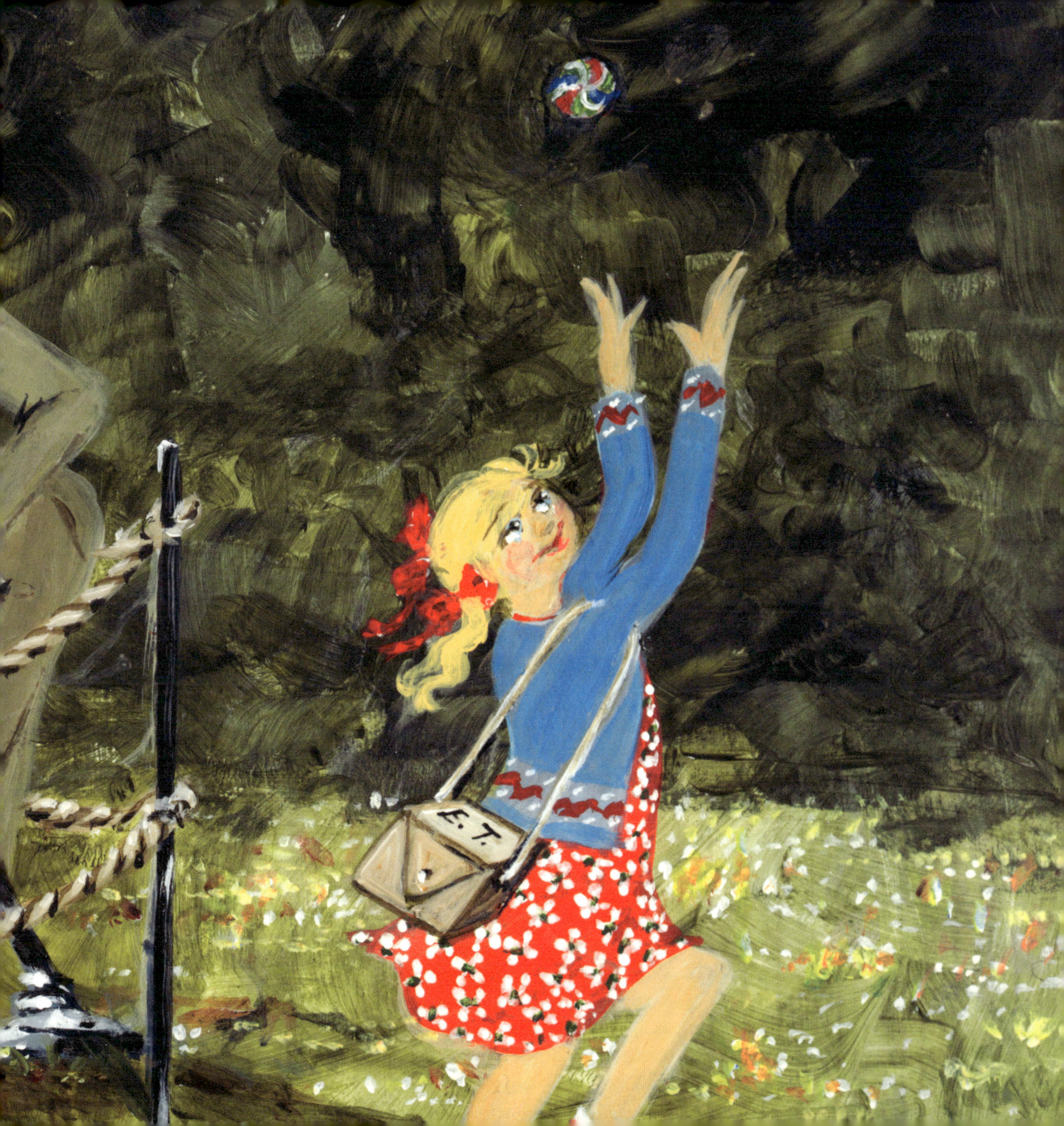
E.T.

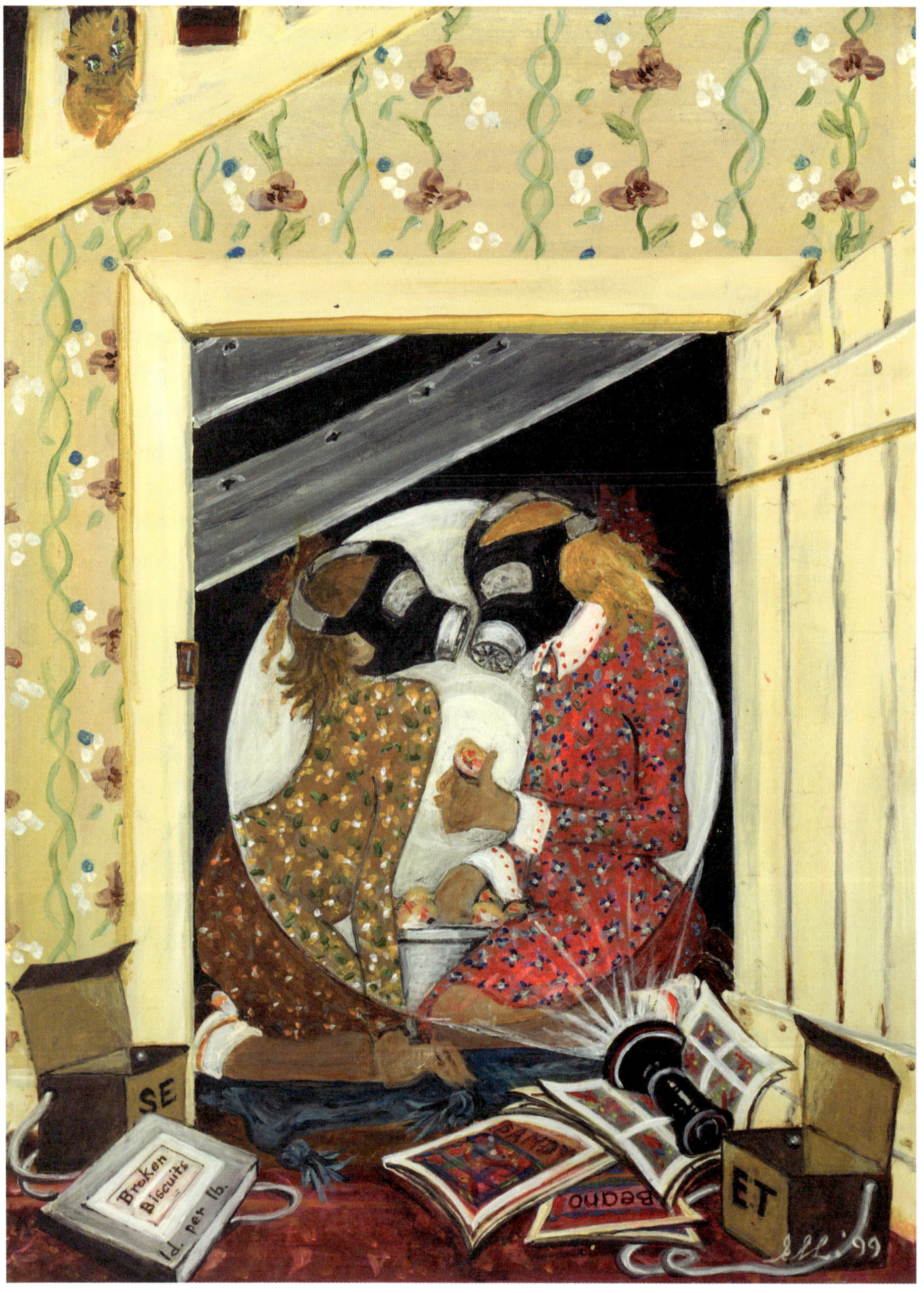

SE
Broken Biscuits
½d. per lb.
Beano
ET

SO HOW DO WE EAT THESE?

Whilst at school we were allocated air-raid shelters spread out in a radius around the building and were to march there in twos, hand in hand, as soon as we heard the air raid warning, the wailing sound of urgency making our hair stand on end. I was lucky in my billet nearby, for it was a grocer's. My partner and I were welcomed with big smiles and warm hugs, then sent to their reinforced under-the-stairs with a big rusty tin of broken biscuits, some of them delicious, given us whilst awaiting the all-clear siren. Our stomachs felt very full, if not sick, by the time we got back to school.

RAISING MONEY FOR SPITFIRES

Railings and gates disappeared overnight from parks, and any other area bounded by iron or steel, for we were short of Spitfires to drive off the hordes of bombers and fighters with only one goal in mind: the invasion and conquering of Britain. Thus, a campaign was launched to raise money to make more Spitfires in a hurry. Every street in the land joined in, raising money in every way we could think of. I got a Spitfire badge for raising something like £20 by painting twigs white and selling them around the doors for decoration.

There were apples from Gu's farm, a children's library pushed round in a wooden box on wheels, made by my brother, and concerts held in our garage, the boldest of us singing a song, reciting a poem or doing a dance. There was a mounting and tangible sense of urgency, if not panic, but all efforts were rewarded when the Luftwaffe finally gave up this first massive Blitzing of our towns and cities, beaten hollow by our Royal Air Force in the Battle of Britain, the Spitfire becoming a legend in history.

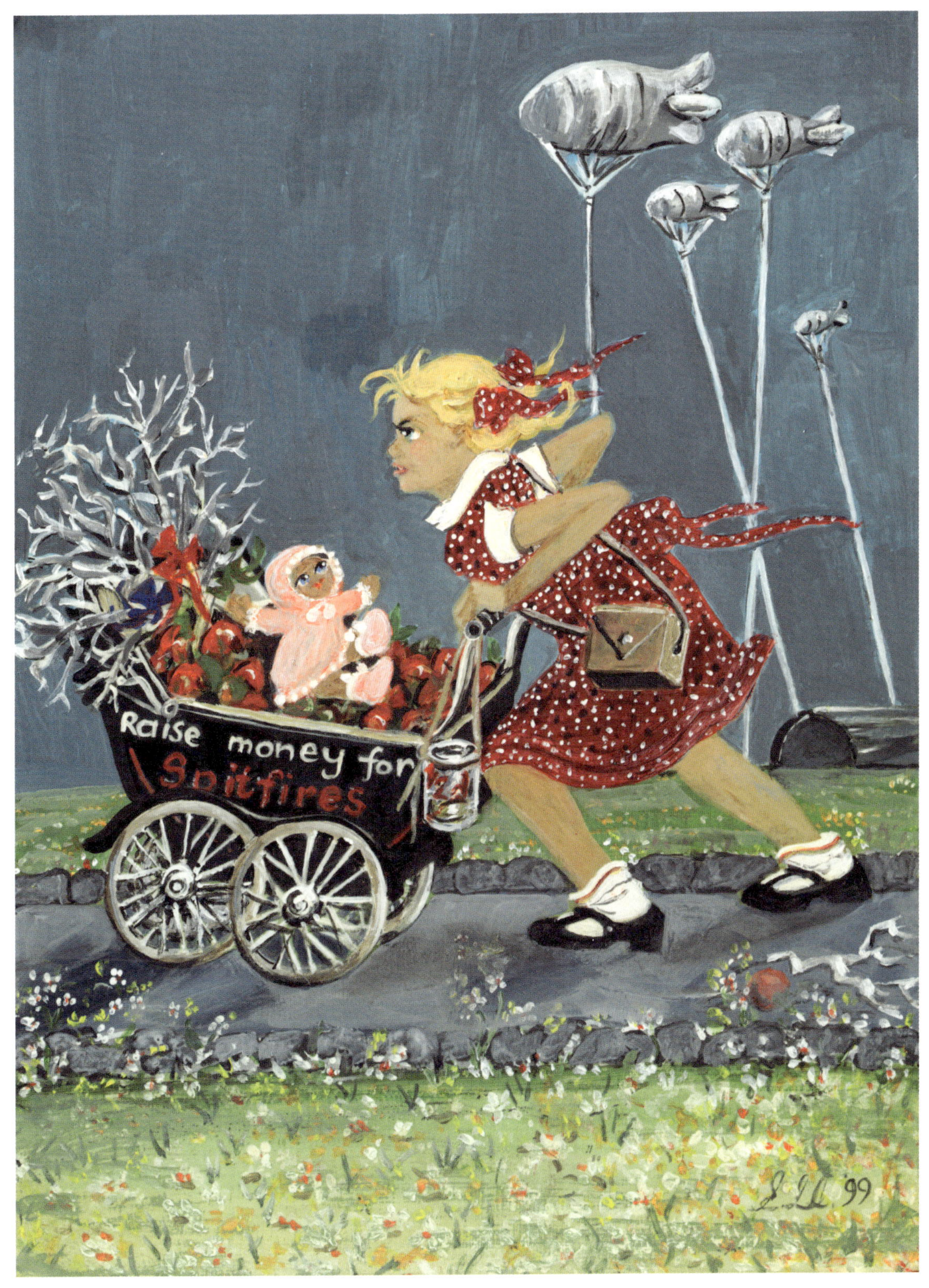

Raise money for
Spitfires

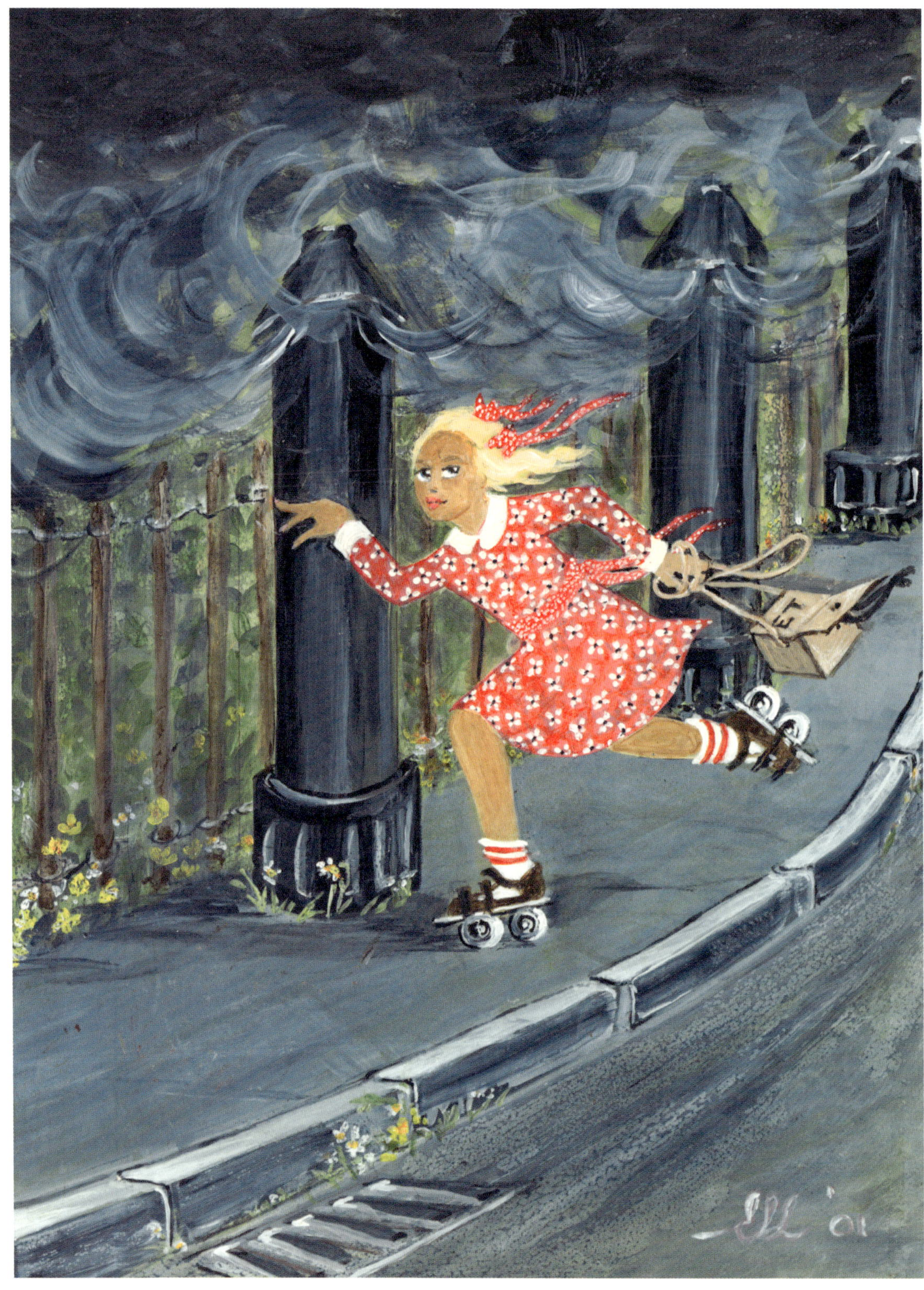

SMOKESCREEN

During the war, we children were issued with gas-masks as protection from mustard gas, a very nasty substance that could blind and choke us, even kill us.

Teachers fitted each one of us, adjusting straps to make us as comfortable as possible, but nothing worked. The celluloid eyepiece misted up, meaning that we couldn't see, and we could hardly breathe through the filters in the nosepiece. Folded up, the masks fitted easily into brown cardboard boxes with a long string strap to hang from our shoulders.

It was babies I was sorry for, their prams encased in a big contraption with a concertina-like pipe. They used to yell their heads off inside, their mothers meanwhile mopping their own tears at such a state of affairs, such a brutal intrusion into their previously safe and happy lives.

SANTA FLIES IN

My first Christmas party on the R.A.F. camp was another depressing experience, despite Father Christmas turning up in a Spitfire. We children were allowed to climb on the wing and taking it in turns to sit in the cockpit. It was a long drop down into a tiny black hole, and everything was covered with think, black, smelly oil, including the instrument panel. Every surface was dented and battered, demonstrating that the plane had been in intensive warfare, but the worse thing to me was the smell of cordite, reminding me of the brutal, anguishing death of living things and the day my uncles on the farm took out their guns and shot dead beautiful wild rabbits by the dozen. I left the Christmas party then, inclined to throw my gift-wrapped present over a hedge.

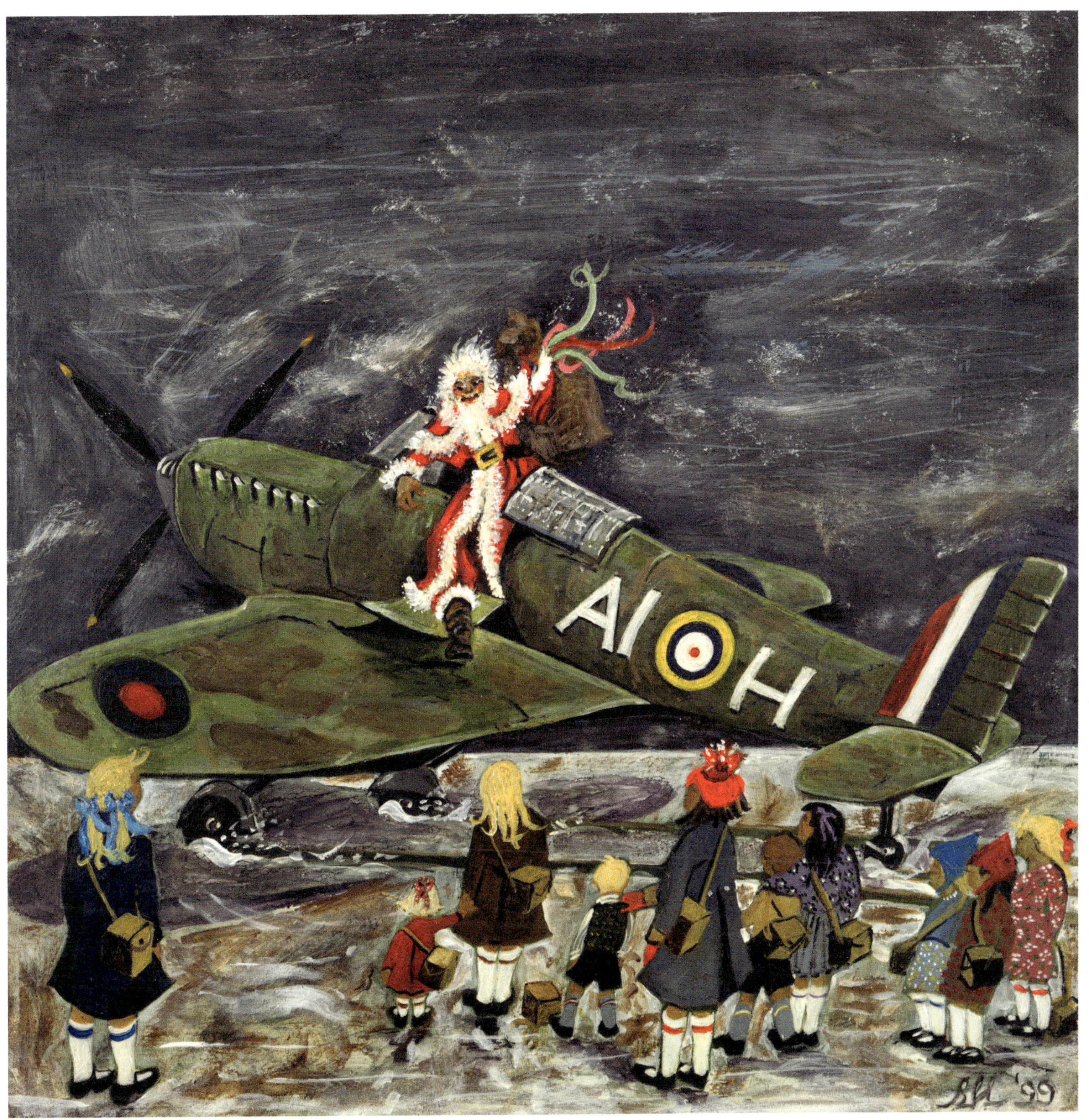

AI◦H

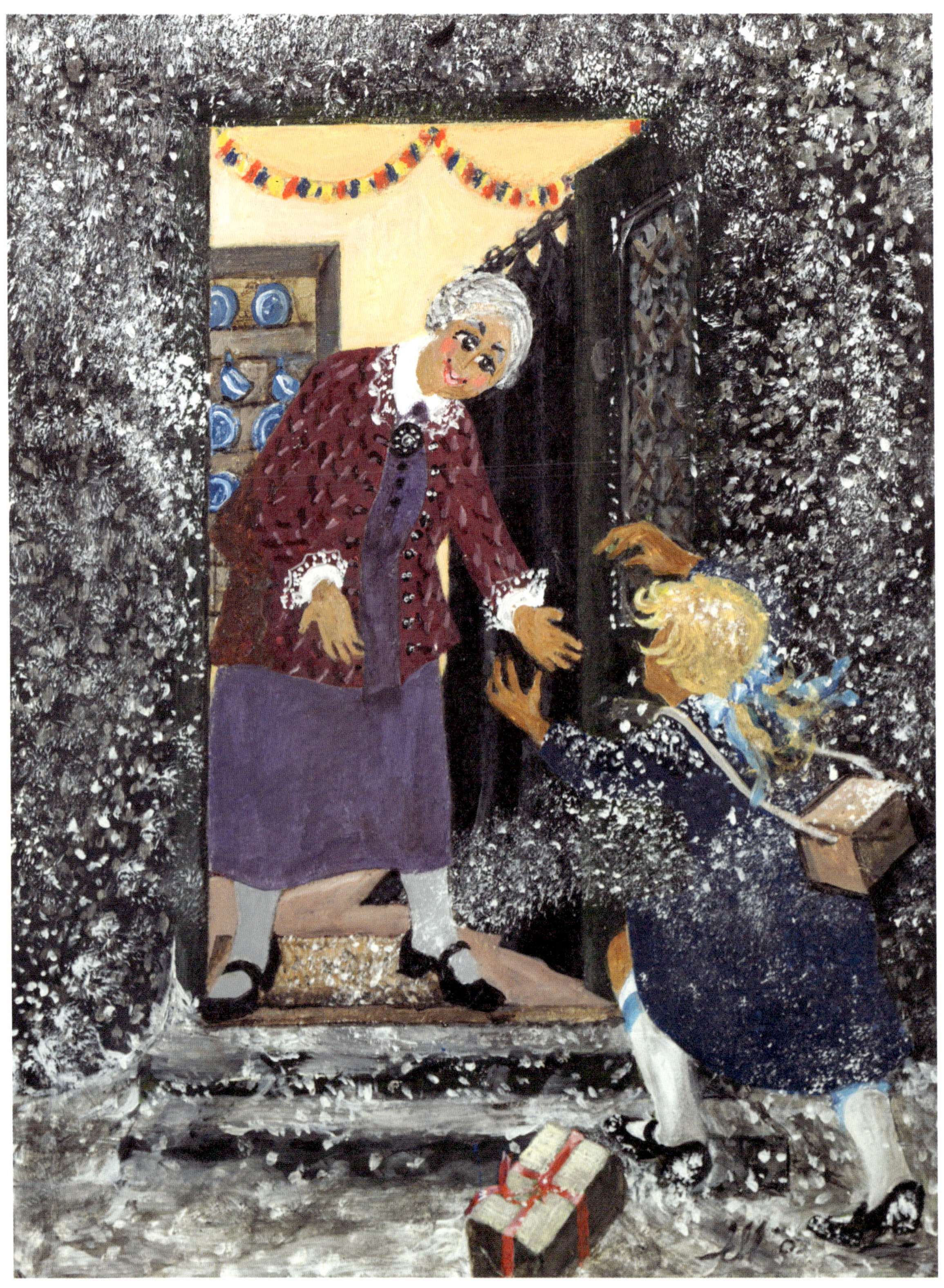

AUNTY NELLIE COMES FOR CHRISTMAS

On Christmas Eve, when I approached my home, the door burst open and who should be standing there but my beloved merry spinster aunt, Aunty Nellie. She had travelled all day by bus to spend Christmas with this cut off branch of the family. To me, this was a gift surpassing gold, frankincense and myrrh.

Thus, I moved onto the next bleak years of World War II, reassured that it would not last forever, and that we would win. We did.

G.I. JOE WWII

This was just a few days before the D-Day landings, and I was still living on the RAF camp, where my father was based. Pitched across the base were many American soldiers, camped out. They would give us oranges and chewing gum, throwing these precious treats to us from the back of their trucks as we cycled behind, which was great fun.

One GI in particular would talk to me through the wire mesh of the fencing as I walked by (I think he thought I was older than I was). He invited me to a film showing on the camp, which was marvellous to me, and off we went that evening. My father would have been furious had he known, me being only fourteen, but I looked older.

Our outing was innocent and joyous and lifted my spirits more than I could say. I couldn't wait to see him again and to listen to his accent as we talked. He was handsome and very polite and interested to hear all about me, which meant a great deal to me.

Discovering that the GIs had shipped out, gone, not a tent peg left where they had camped, shook me profoundly. I couldn't believe my eyes that so many people, so much hubbub, could just disappear overnight. These brave young men were, of course, part of the D-Day landings, where so many lost their lives.

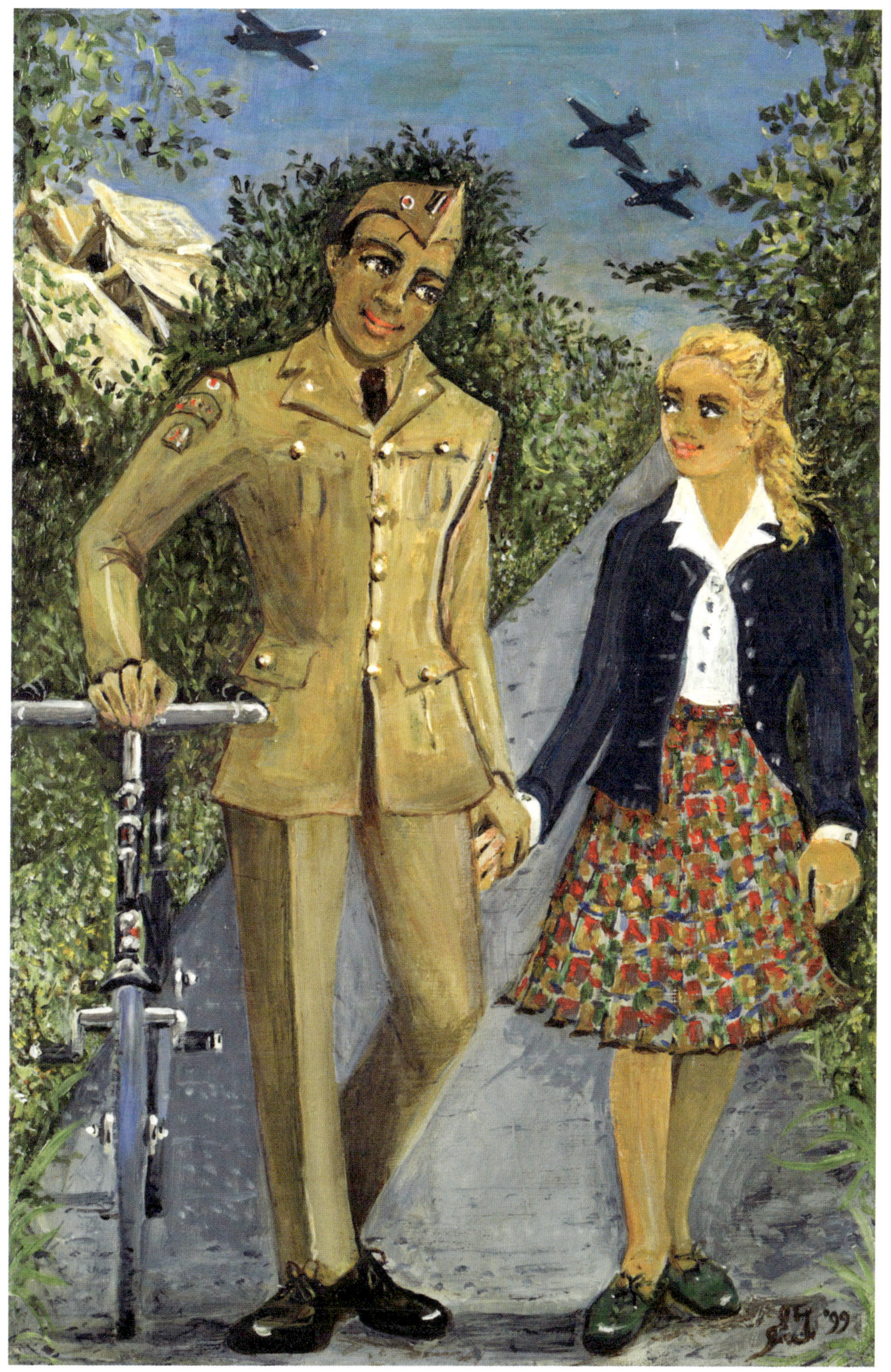

EIRONWY LLEWELLYN

Born in 1930 in Aberystwyth, Wales, Eironwy Llewellyn was a free spirit and would love seeing her work shared with the world. Her headstone reads: 'May the sun always shine on your dear face, the grass always be green under your feet, the wind in your hair.'

She trained at Swansea College of Art (1946-1951), receiving the National Diploma in Design in Modelling & Sculpture and Art Teacher Diploma. Eironwy was also an associate member of the British Association of Art Therapists.

These original paintings, painted retrospectively whilst in her seventies, are a pictorial diary of her childhood in Wales from 1930-1944, the jaunty, naive style conveying her life as remembered 'through the eyes of a child'.

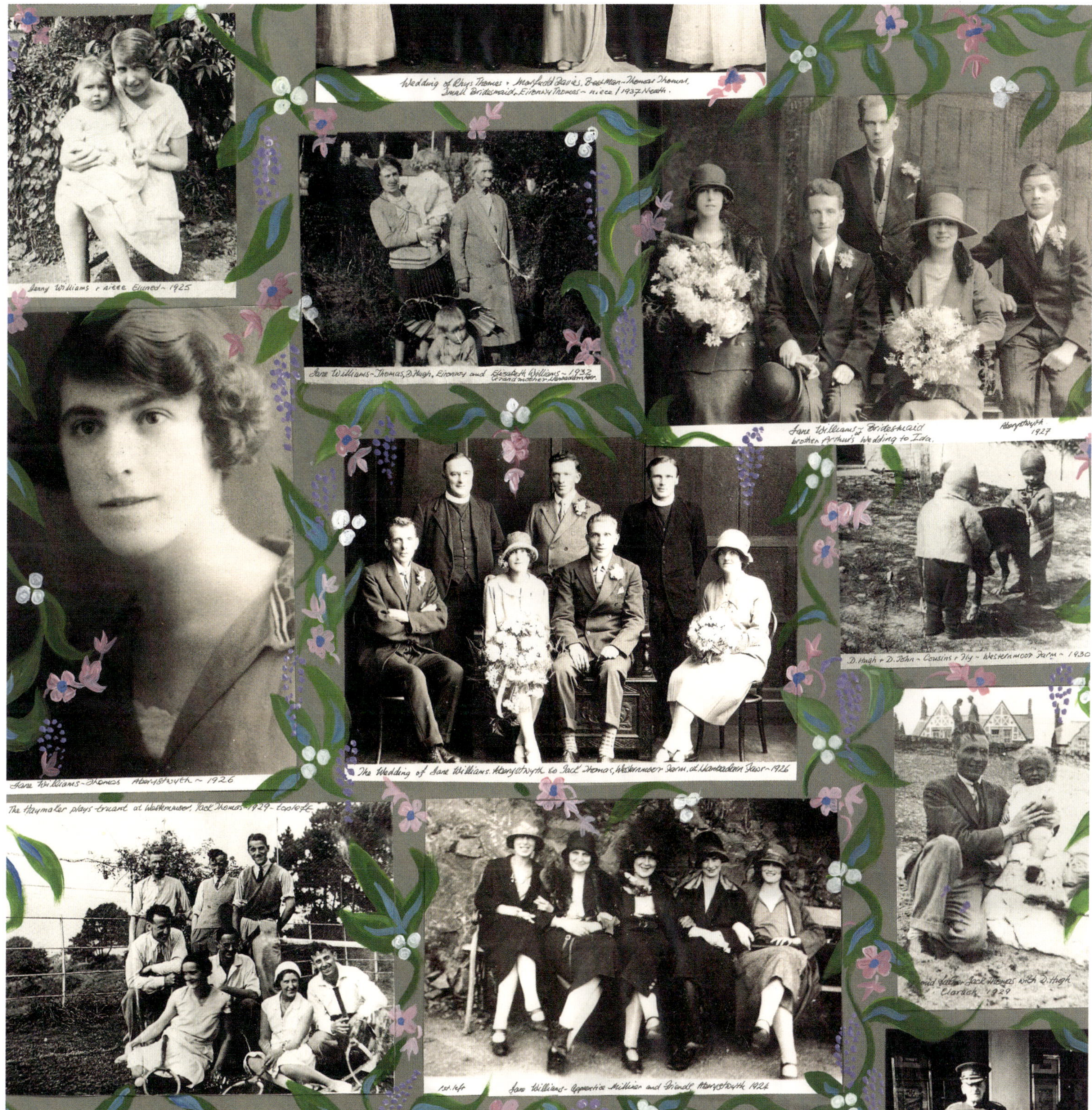
Wedding of Rhys Thomas & Morfudd Davies, Best Man~Thomas Thomas. Small Bridesmaid, Eleanor Thomas~niece. 1937 Neath.
Jenny Williams & niece Eluned~1925
Jane Williams~Thomas, D. Hugh, Eleanor and Elizabeth Williams~1932 Grandmother~Llanbadarn Fawr.
Jane Williams & Bridesmaid, brother Arthur's Wedding to Ivor. Aberystwyth 1927
Jane Williams~Thomas Aberystwyth~1926
The Wedding of Jane Williams. Aberystwyth to Jack Thomas, Westernmoor Farm, at Llanbadarn Fawr~1926
D. Hugh & D. John~Cousins & Fly~Westernmoor Farm~1930
Proud father Jack Thomas with D. Hugh Clarach 1929
The Haymaker plays truant at Westernmoor, Jack Thomas 1929~top left.
1st. left   Jane Williams~Apprentice Milliner and Friends, Aberystwyth 1926

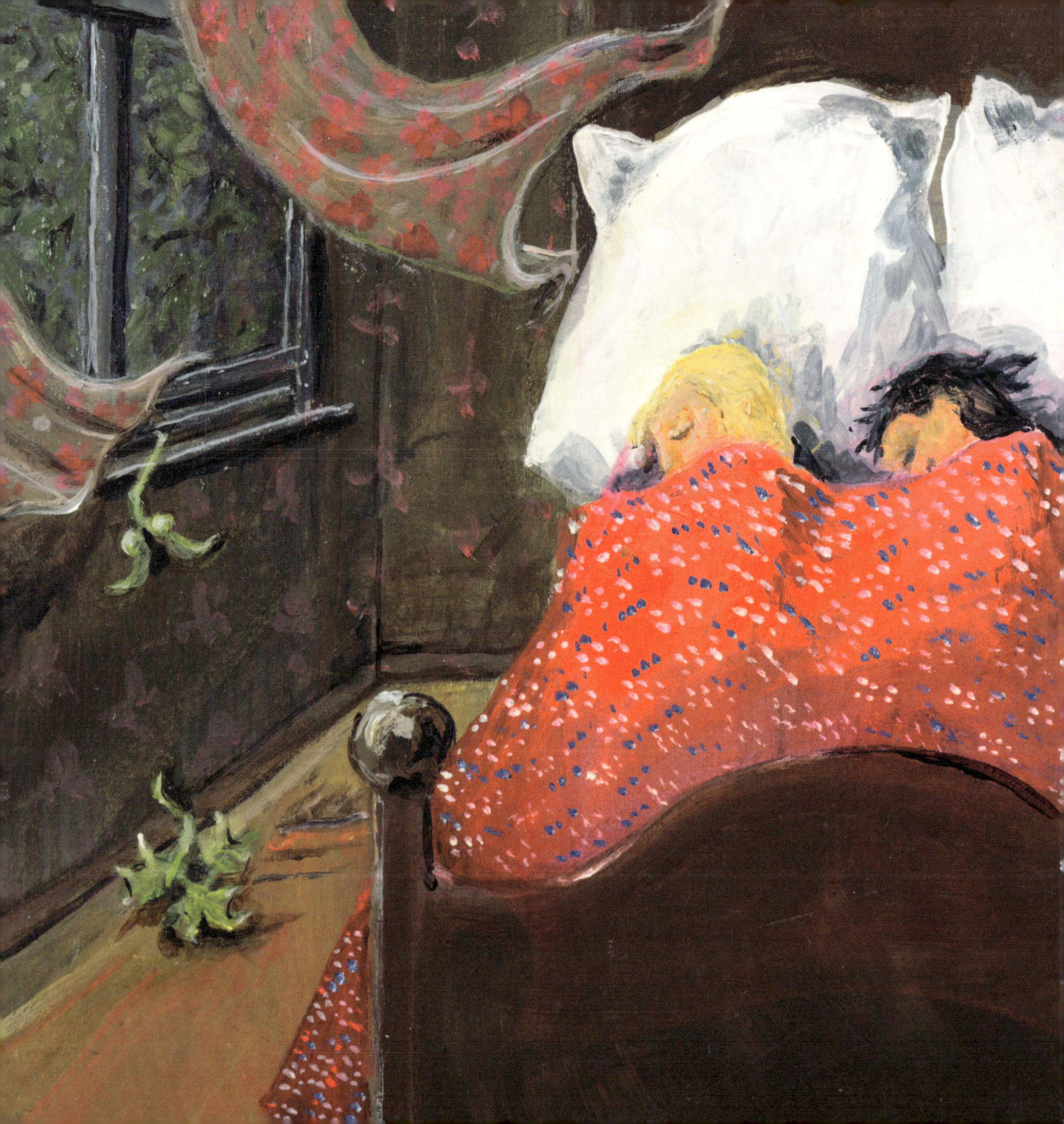